RYA National Sailing Scheme Instructor Handbook

Revised and Updated February 2012
Reprinted October 2012
Revised and Updated October 2013

© RYA National Sailing Scheme Instructor Handbook
Copyright RYA 2011

The Royal Yachting Association
RYA House, Ensign Way,
Hamble, Southampton,
Hampshire SO31 4YA

Tel: 0844 556 9555
Fax: 0844 556 9516
E-mail: publications@rya.org.uk
Web: www.rya.org.uk

ISBN 978-1-906435-52-3
RYA Order Code G14

Technical Editing

Amanda Van Santen, Laurence West, Grahame Forshaw.

Contributions

Mike Hart, Andy Carley, Nic Wymer, Debbie Blatchford, Simon Davies, David Ritchie, John Thorn.

Photo Credits

Laurence West, Grahame Forshaw, Richard Langdon/Ocean Images.

The RYA is committed to encouraging both men and women to participate in sailing. For clarity only, this book is written using the masculine gender e.g. man overboard.

A CIP record of this book is available from the British Library.
Ring 0844 556 9555 for a free copy of our Publications Catalogue.

Totally Chlorine Free   Sustainable Forests   EMAS VERIFIED ENVIRONMENTAL MANAGEMENT

Published by **The Royal Yachting Association**
RYA House, Ensign Way, Hamble, Southampton SO31 4YA
Tel: 0844 556 9555
Fax: 0844 556 9516
Email: publications@rya.org.uk
Web: www.rya.org.uk
Follow us on Twitter @RYAPublications

Note: While all reasonable care has been taken in the preparation of this book, the publisher takes no responsibility for the use of the methods or products or contracts described in the book.

Illustrators: Doug Bishenden, Richard Lloyd, Phil Twining and Jake Kavanagh.
Cover design: Jude Williams
Typeset: Jude Williams
Printed by: Printed in China through World Print

Contents

Contents

Foreword

Sailing is a wonderfully diverse sport with so many types of boats to suit everyone, regardless of age or ability. The RYA National Sailing Scheme offers one of the best ways into the sport and the progressive training programme, made up of a series of two day courses, enables participants to progress quickly from beginner to expert in a controlled, safe and fun environment.

Participants can choose to learn in dinghies, multihulls or small keelboats, offering a level of activity and adrenaline to suit any taste.

The Youth Sailing Scheme is closely aligned to the adult National Sailing Scheme, but with even more emphasis on fun and games in the early stages. It is delivered in smaller bite sized chunks to build confidence and skills.

Both the youth and the adult schemes offer parallel routes through learning the basics before embarking on the more advanced courses, where more specialist skills are taught and individual coaching is provided.

The RYA sailing schemes are taught in a vast number of locations from the open sea to small lakes, from the north of Scotland to the shores of the Mediterranean. The boats vary from Optimists and Picos to keelboats and multihulls. In spite of this variation, the process of learning to sail has remained largely unchanged during the forty plus years that the RYA has run a national training scheme.

The RYA method known to every dinghy instructor has stood the test of time with few modifications and remains as effective today as it was at its inception. This book explains the techniques and progressions that make up the method along with all the other skills and knowledge required by RYA instructors. It assumes you are already a competent sailor who would like to become involved in an RYA training centre, teaching dinghy, multihull or keelboat sailing.

This instructor handbook is for all those working, or volunteering, as instructors, senior instructors and coaches within the RYA National Sailing Scheme and Youth Sailing Scheme. This publication also includes an explanation of who can teach the scheme and where, and space to include your log of instructional experience and courses attended.

Amanda Van Santen
Chief Instructor – Dinghy & Windsurfing

2 | Equal Opportunities

POLICY STATEMENT

The RYA is committed to the principle of equality of opportunity and aims to ensure that all present and potential participants, members, instructors, coaches, competitors, officials, volunteers and employees are treated fairly and on an equal basis, irrespective of sex, age, disability, race, colour, religion or belief, sexual orientation, pregnancy and maternity, marriage and civil partnerships, gender reassignment or social status.

Objectives

- To make boating an activity that is genuinely open to anyone who wishes to take part.
- To provide the framework for everyone to enjoy the sport, in whatever capacity and to whatever level the individual desires.
- To ensure that the RYA's services, including training schemes, are accessible to all, including those who have been under-represented in the past.

Implementation

- The RYA encourages its affiliated clubs and organisations and its recognised training centres to adopt a similar policy, so that they are seen as friendly, welcoming and open to all.
- Appointments to voluntary or paid positions with the RYA will be made on the basis of an individual's knowledge, skills and experience and the competences required for the role.
- The RYA will relax regulations in relation to RYA training schemes which may inhibit the performance of candidates with special needs, provided that the standard, quality and integrity of schemes and assessments are not compromised.
- The RYA reserves the right to discipline any of its members or employees who practise any form of discrimination in breach of this policy.
- The effectiveness of this policy will be monitored and evaluated on an ongoing basis.

RYA TRAINING CENTRES

RYA recognised training centres can issue RYA certificates in the disciplines for which they have been approved. These centres fall into three main categories:

* Sailing centres open to the public.
* Sailing clubs providing tuition for their members and prospective members.
* Organisations such as local education authorities, Scouts and HM Services, teaching their own groups or members.

RYA training centre recognition is vested in the Principal. They are responsible for issuing RYA certificates and ensuring that the requirements of RYA recognition are maintained at all times.

Guidelines for the recognition of RYA training centres are available in a separate document from the RYA or from the website at www.rya.org.uk.

RYA AFFILIATED CLUBS

Affiliated clubs have been at the very heart of the RYA since its foundation in 1875, and a large part of RYA work is still devoted to their promotion and protection. Any club with an RYA-specified boating interest may apply to the RYA for affiliation, namely:

* Windsurfing.
* Dinghy Sailing (cruising and racing).
* Yacht Sailing (cruising and racing).
* Motor cruising.
* Sportsboats and RIBs.
* Personal watercraft.
* Powerboat racing.
* Inland waterways.

It is normally a requirement that a club applying for affiliation has at least 30 members. For full affiliation, a club must have democratically elected officers and a constitution showing that no outside body has control over its affairs. Fully affiliated clubs have one vote for each £1 of affiliation fees paid in voting rights on RYA matters. Clubs that cannot demonstrate democratic process or independence may apply for restricted affiliation, a separate category with no voting rights. For further information about becoming affiliated to the RYA or the benefits of doing so, please contact the RYA at info@rya.org.uk.

RYA CHAMPION CLUBS

The RYA Champion Club Programme accredits and supports those clubs that have made a commitment to put the development of Junior Racing at the forefront of club activity. They are safe and effective places to develop your skills and there will almost certainly be one in your area. Team 15 clubs encompass the same values but focus on the windsurfing rather than dinghy sailing. The process is run by the RYA High Performance Managers. All details are listed in the RYA website.

A Champion Club is required to:

* Provide a structured Junior Race Training Programme
* Guide their promising youngsters into the recognised youth classes following their period in a junior class.
* Have sufficient numbers of a recognised junior class of boat (members or club owned), equipment and qualified personnel to achieve the aims of partnership.

3 | RYA Organisations

ONBOARD

Sailing and windsurfing are fun and give young people an early opportunity to develop confidence, independence and a sense of purpose. But it's not always easy to get started. OnBoard is a nationwide programme that is making it easier for young people to go sailing and windsurfing and get involved in a variety of local activities. It is co-ordinated by the RYA, supported by industry and the sports, and delivered locally by RYA Training Centres. Over a ten year period the programme aims to introduce a minimum of 500,000 children to sailing and windsurfing in the UK; with more than 10% of them becoming regular participants.

We want more young people to be able to join in the fun of sailing and windsurfing and take up the opportunities to stay involved in our sports. To find out more about OnBoard visit www.ruob.co.uk.

THE DUKE OF EDINBURGH'S AWARD

The RYA is recognised as a National Operating Authority for The Duke of Edinburgh's Award (DofE). The DofE is a voluntary, non-competitive programme of activities for anyone aged 14 to 24, giving the opportunity to experience new activities or develop existing skills.

There are three progressive levels of programmes which, when successfully completed, lead to a Bronze, Silver or Gold Award.

Doing your DofE

Achieving a DofE Award can be made an adventure from beginning to end. Within an RYA club or training centre, there are already so many activities young people could take part in which can count towards their DofE. These could range from:

- **Volunteering**: Helping out at your local Training Centre, club or Team 15 night on a regular basis, this could be as an assistant, in the kitchen or maybe even on the committee!
- **Physical**: Regularly taking part in Sailing or windsurfing activity, why not set yourself a goal to gain a certain certificate in the RYA National Sailing or Windsurfing scheme or maybe participate in regular club racing.
- **Skill**: All about developing your skills, whether practical, social or personal. You may choose to sharpen up your powerboating, learn a new skill such as boat repair work, become an instructor or perhaps increase your theory knowledge and learn all about meteorology!
- **Residential and Expedition**: You may never have been away from home before, let alone using your board or boat to go on an exciting adventure with friends, so now is the time!

DofE Timescales:

BRONZE (14+ years)			
VOLUNTEERING	**PHYSICAL**	**SKILLS**	**EXPEDITION**
3 months	3 months	3 months	Plan, train for and undertake a 2 day, 1 night expedition
All participants must undertake a further 3 months in the Volunteering, Physical or Skills sections			

Silver (15+ years)			
VOLUNTEERING	**PHYSICAL**	**SKILLS**	**EXPEDITION**
6 months	3 Once section for 6 months and the other section for 3 months	Plan, train for and undertake a 3 day, 2 night expedition	Plan, train for and undertake a 3 day, 2 night expedition
Direct entrants must undertake a further 6 months in either the Volunteering or the longer of the Physical or Skills sections.			

Gold (16+ years)			
VOLUNTEERING	**PHYSICAL**	**SKILLS**	**EXPEDITION**
12 months	One section for 12 months and the other section for 6 months	Plan, train for and undertake a 4 day, 3 night expedition	Undertake a shared activity in a residential setting away from home for 5 days and 4 nights.
Direct entrants must undertake a further 6 months in either the Volunteering or the longer of the Physical or Skills sections.			

Getting involved as an Instructor, Coach or Trainer

There is a considerable amount of interaction between the participants and the adults who are supporting them, with specific DofE roles such as Centre Coordinators, Leaders, Supervisors and Assessors. If you are interested in helping, further information on these roles can be found by visiting the DofE website.

Further information can be found, explaining the opportunities available, on the DofE website www.dofe.org, and the RYA website www.rya.org.uk/go/dofe.

4 | General Considerations

DUTY OF CARE

Instructors and Coaches must always remember that they are usually teaching relatively inexperienced sailors, who may not be able to make a sound assessment of the risks inherent in the sport. Instructors and particularly Senior Instructors should not hesitate to make prudent decisions in unfavourable conditions to ensure the safety of the students in their care.

INSTRUCTOR HEALTH DECLARATION

RYA Instructors and Coaches must declare any medical condition which might affect their duty of care as an instructor. They also undertake to inform the RYA of any relevant change in their medical situation after qualifying.

The RYA reserves the right to withhold or suspend qualification from anyone who is considered unlikely to fulfil this requirement.

STUDENT HEALTH DECLARATION

In order that they are informed as to any additional risk to students, RYA training centres are strongly advised to include a health declaration in their booking forms. The Principal/Chief Instructor must pass on such information to the individual instructor responsible for the student.

The declaration should say that the student is, to the best of their knowledge, not suffering from epilepsy, disability, giddy spells, asthma, angina or other heart condition, and is fit to participate in the course. It should be signed and dated by the student and include details of any medical conditions or injuries and medication being taken. If there is doubt as to someone's fitness to take part, medical advice may be sought.

SWIMMERS

It is recommended that all those participating in the sport of sailing should be able to swim.
No minimum level swimming ability is stipulated, but students should be able to demonstrate water confidence. It is essential that the instructor in charge of a course knows if any course members are non-swimmers. Non-swimmers may be required to wear life jackets instead of buoyancy aids.

RYA Coach Assessor

RYA Senior Instructor

Keelboat/Multihull/Dinghy Instructor Endorsements

| **RYA Advanced Instructor Endorsement** | ⬅ | **RYA Instructor** | ⇨ | **RYA Racing Instructor Endorsement (RCL1)** |

RYA Assistant Instructor

RYA ASSISTANT INSTRUCTOR

The Assistant Instructor is trained to assist qualified instructors to teach beginners up to the standard of the National Sailing Scheme Level 2 and the Youth Sailing Scheme Stage 3. They must only work under the supervision of a Senior Instructor. The award is centre specific.

Role

- Assists RYA Instructors.
- Instructs up to National Sailing Certificate Level 2 and Stage 3 of the Youth Sailing Scheme.

Eligibility for the Training Course

- Sailing Standard – Pass one of the National Sailing Scheme Advanced Modules.
- Recommendation by Principal of training centre.

Training

Training will cover the centre's safe operating procedures and the teaching points related to teaching beginners shown later in this book.

The award is centre specific. Training is based on a two day (or modular) course of 20 hrs duration at the centre, run by the Principal/Chief Instructor who holds a valid RYA Senior Instructor certificate.

Assessment

Candidates will be assessed on their practical teaching ability with beginners. Successful candidates will be awarded an RYA Assistant Instructor certificate by their Principal.

Certificate Validity

The centre specific Assistant Instructor certificate is awarded to successful candidates by their training centre and is valid for five years.

Assistant Instructor Training Course

- Attend either a specific training course over 20 hrs, or receive 1:1 'on-the-job' training over a similar period.
- Training is primarily afloat covering teaching points from each session.
- Will be based around the centre's main fleet (double or single handers).
- If double handers, the AI will helm initially then hand over to the students as quickly as possible.
- If single handers, the AI will mainly be a helper, rigger, catcher etc.
- After training, AI candidates will be assessed on their ability to teach beginners effectively.

Important Note

The AI does not need to hold a first aid or powerboat certificate, therefore AIs must never be allowed to work without direct supervision.

The award is centre specific. Thus if an Assistant Instructor moves from one training centre to another, it is likely that his new Principal will issue a new Assistant Instructor Award after retraining.

RYA INSTRUCTOR PRE-ENTRY SAILING ASSESSMENT

Before being accepted onto an instructor training course, candidates need to pass this assessment of sailing skills. This is a practical test conducted by an RYA Coach/Assessor not more than one year in advance of their proposed course. This will determine whether they have the required sailing ability to become an instructor, as there is little time on the course for training input to improve their sailing skills.

It is recommended that, prior to taking the assessment, candidates satisfy themselves that they can sail confidently and to the standard detailed below. They should also have the appropriate background knowledge and understanding of requirements.

During the assessment, the candidate will be judged on his preparation for and execution of each of the tasks, including awareness of others. The assessment will be made in a boat of the candidate's or coach's choice, with a Portsmouth Yardstick of less than 1230. If the assessment is conducted in a keelboat or multihull, the rudderless sailing section should be omitted.

The assessment may be undertaken during a skills course run by an RYA Coach/Assessor. Candidates for a coastal instructor certificate should undertake the sailing assessment on coastal waters.

The candidate should be able to complete the following tasks, sailing at all times with an awareness of 'the Five Essentials' i.e. sail setting, balance, trim, centreboard and course sailed. The Assessor will be seeking to confirm that the candidate can sail in a controlled and competent manner, considering preparation, communication, approach and execution for each exercise.

1 Sail around a triangular course

- Each leg of the course will be a minimum of 100 metres.
- Close mark rounding.
- Allow for tide if appropriate.
- Use all the boat's equipment to best advantage including spinnaker if carried.

2 Sail a tight circular course

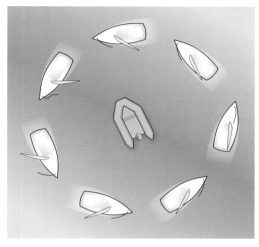

- Circle less than three boat lengths' radius around a stationary (free floating) boat.
- Make only one tack and one gybe.
- Sail trim and boat balance/trim suited to the manoeuvre.

The circle should be as small as you can safely make it, but the Assessor will accept that, in doing this, you might have to leave the centreboard in one position.

3 Sail a follow-my-leader course

- On all points of sailing.
- Speeding up/slowing down (up and down wind).
- Maintain a constant distance (1-2 boat lengths).

4 Pick up a man overboard dummy

- Boat must be stopped dead in the water when you pick up the dummy.
- Pick up at the windward shroud.
- Do not tack while you pull it aboard.
- Pick up on the first attempt.

You may also be asked to complete some of the following:

1 Sail rudderless, or with rudder in place and the tiller on loose elastic (class dependent)

- Sail a triangular course.

- Demonstrate effective sail trim/boat balance.
- Modifications to sail area, sheeting purchase and centreboard setting are permitted during the exercise.
- Consider other water users and apply the 'Rules of the road'.

2 Lee shore landing and departure

- Use correct sail plan, jib only if necessary.
- Land in a controlled fashion.
- On departure, clear the shore successfully in a controlled way on the first attempt.

3 Pick up a mooring or anchor

- Correct sail plan.
- Boat should be stopped next to the buoy.
- Pick up buoy first time.
- When mooring buoy is on board, the boat should remain under control.
- Anchoring to take place in the area designated by the Assessor.
- Anchoring should be successful on the first attempt.
- After the anchor has held, the boat should remain under control.

4 Come alongside a moored boat

- Approach under control.
- Stop alongside on the first attempt.
- Remain in control thereafter.

The Coach/Assessor will use an appropriate selection of these exercises to make a judgement of the candidate. Preparation and execution of the task will be judged as well as the factoring in of an 'escape' route. He will use the tasks most suited to the location and conditions.

Throughout this section the phrase 'on the first attempt' should not be taken to mean that you cannot make a seamanlike decision to break off at a reasonably early stage and try again. It merely means that once you have become committed to a task, it should be successfully completed.

5 Recover a capsized dinghy and sail away

- Recover the dinghy on the first attempt.
- No external help permitted.
- The recovery should be controlled and seamanlike.
- Ensure that the boat and the candidates are fully prepared for the event.

Throughout the pre-entry sailing assessment, the Coach/Assessor will try to obtain an overall impression of your sailing ability and whether it is of the required RYA standard. As a result, you might technically fail one task and still pass the assessment. The Coach/Assessor may also take into account previous sailing experience.

You should not attempt the pre-entry assessment without practising all the tasks in the boat in which you or the Assessor intends you to use to take the test, or one similar.

Finally, please remember that although the pre-entry is likely to be conducted in a double handed dinghy, the instructor course will include practical work in single handlers. All instructors are therefore expected to be capable of sailing the single handers commonly used within training centres such as Picos, Toppers and Lasers. Any instructor candidate unfamiliar with these boats is recommended to gain some experience of them prior to the training course.

RYA DINGHY/KEELBOAT/MULTIHULL INSTRUCTOR

It is possible to complete the National Sailing Scheme in dinghies, keelboats or multihulls. Therefore instructors teaching the scheme must be qualified for the type of boat in which they will be teaching i.e. only RYA Dinghy Instructors can teach in dinghies, and only RYA Keelboat Instructors can teach in keelboats although Dinghy Instructors can broaden their qualification to include keelboats and vice versa. The instructor certificate is endorsed accordingly and will also show whether the instructor is qualified to teach on inland or coastal waters (depending on where they completed the pre-entry sailing assessment and course).

Role

- Competent, experienced sailor able to sail in strong winds.
- Qualified powerboat handler to RYA Powerboat Level 2.
- Can teach in dinghies, keelboats or multihulls depending on previous experience and training.
- Can teach RYA National Sailing Scheme Levels 1, 2, 3, Seamanship Skills, Day Sailing, Sailing with Spinnakers (where appropriately experienced and approved by the centre principal) and Youth Sailing Scheme Stages 1-4.

Eligibility for the Training Course

- Minimum age 16 (no candidates will be accepted for training under this age).
- A valid RYA First Aid certificate, or another acceptable first aid qualification as detailed on the RYA website (www.rya.org.uk/go/firstaidcertificates).
- RYA Powerboat Level 2 certificate.
- Pre-entry sailing assessment completed within one year prior to the instructor training course.
- RYA membership

Training

Throughout your training, it is important to remember that the RYA teaching methods used have been developed successfully over many years. You will be introduced to some techniques which have become standardised because it is important that RYA instruction should follow broadly the same pattern in every training centre.

It is equally important, however, that you should not follow certain drills slavishly without considering that certain boats will require variations of the 'method'. Without scope for minor variations, there would be no room for development and improvement.

- Course staffed by RYA Coaches/Assessors.
- Training includes teaching techniques ashore and afloat.
- Course duration is normally 50hrs/5 day week but could be modular over a number of weekends or single days. This approach may actually take longer.
- A list of courses running can be obtained from RYA HQ.
- The structure and content of the National Sailing Scheme and Youth Sailing Scheme.
- Training in RYA teaching methods to the Seamanship Skills Module including teaching those with special needs.

- Instructing techniques for adults and children.
- Preparation and presentation of a lesson.
- Preparation and use of visual aids.
- The assessment of students' abilities.
- A form of written paper (or oral test) covering teaching methods and background.
- The use of powered craft in a teaching environment.
- Safeguarding, child protection, Health & Safety, and cold water shock.

Throughout the course, evidence of competence in these areas will be noted by the training Coach/Assessor and credited towards the candidate's final moderation/assessment.

RYA Instructor Course Moderation/ Assessment

Certificate Validity

- Instructor certificates valid for 5 years from date of issue if supported by a valid first aid certificate.
- Certificates can be revalidated by obtaining and returning a completed revalidation form accompanied by a log of teaching experience in an RYA training centre, valid first aid certificate, valid RYA membership number or appropriate fee.
- A minimum of 30 hours' teaching experience is required.
- Little or no logged experience may require a re-assessment to ensure the instructor is still up to date.
- Revalidation should normally include all existing instructor endorsements.

Instructor courses are moderated by an outside moderator (coach/assessor) who has not been involved in the training. Their task is to confirm that all RYA standards expected on the course have been upheld by the training coach and the candidates and they will do this partly by observing the candidates deliver teaching in as realistic conditions as possible.

The moderation will follow the pattern below:

- Moderation will take place immediately following the training course.
- Moderation elements will include practical teaching afloat, a teaching session ashore, teaching a land drill and giving a short 5 minute presentation (optional).
- Your training coach will take the role of the Senior Instructor and outline the order of the day to you.
- If possible, there may be 'real students' to teach.
- If teaching in a double hander, it is likely that the moderator will join you in the boat.
- They are able to form an accurate opinion in a short time, so don't be concerned if they don't spend long with you.
- In the unlikely event that a candidate is not considered ready to be moderated, a separate time for moderation will be suggested, along with an action plan.

The moderator will be looking for:

- The ability to plan the session according to the needs of your students.
- A friendly, supportive manner towards your students, from their arrival to departure.
- Briefing and debriefing skills.
- The boat rigged according to weather conditions and the abilities of your students.
- Adequate boat control at all times.
- Teaching according to the methods outlined on your course and in this book, progressing according to the students' abilities.
- Correct positioning of instructor and students.
- Successful demonstrations and clear explanations.
- Correct diagnosis and tactful correction of students' faults.
- Use of lying-to position for crew changes and briefings.
- Running a safe session.

It is far more natural for you to be teaching 'real students', usually beginners, than for another instructor or the moderator to play the role of a student, but if the latter is necessary the moderator will take account of the false situation.

When beginners are used, the moderator will also be assessing you through their reaction, looking for the three key factors which are important for successful teaching:

- Are the students safe?
- Are they enjoying themselves?
- Are they learning anything valuable?

Although all these points are important, safety remains the highest priority.

Five Minute Presentation

During the training course, candidates will have given a presentation on a topic chosen by the training coach and, prior to giving it, will have had training input on how best to deliver it. In order to achieve a definite outcome, the moderator may ask candidates to deliver a short presentation, possibly unprepared, on an aspect of sailing. Candidates may also be asked to deliver a presentation of this type if their initial presentation did not come up to the required standard.

Practical Demonstration of Land Drills

The moderator may expect you to cover land drills for aft and/or centre mainsheet boats. Before doing so, he will have discussed with your training coach the techniques used during the course, in case there are any local differences from the drills outlined in this handbook.

The moderator is not trying to catch you out by minute attention to detail, but he will be looking for:

- A brief explanation of why drills are used.
- Adequate preparation (and explanation) of equipment.
- Good positioning of students.
- Clear accurate demonstrations, both at normal speed and slowly with commentary.
- Ability to identify and correct students' faults.

Overall Assessment

It is usual for a number of candidates to be assessed on the same day and this will result in a period when you are not directly under the attention of the assessor, but he may still be keeping a distant eye on your work.

Throughout the moderation, in addition to considering the detailed points outlined above, the moderator will be making an overall (or holistic) judgement, based on the criteria and measured against his experience of the sport. The qualities sought can be summarised as:

- Enthusiasm for the sport • Confidence in the subject • Teaching ability • Anticipation
- Awareness of safety throughout

At some point, often at the middle of the day, he will seek comments from the training coach, who has been monitoring your progress throughout the course and so has a good idea of your ability. This will help the moderator to take account of any particular circumstances on the day.

The moderator and training coach will review your performance with you. This debrief may include several more questions to ensure that you have sufficient understanding of different aspects of work as an instructor.

Finally, the training coach and moderator will confirm whether or not you have yet proved your competence as an RYA Instructor and complete the necessary paperwork. If for some reason the candidate is not entirely successful then an action plan will be drawn up and agreed to help overcome any gaps in knowledge or ability.

If you disagree with the decision, they will discuss the possibility of a re-assessment or the procedure for appeal to the RYA.

RYA INSTRUCTOR ENDORSEMENTS

An RYA Instructor can teach students the modules Level 1, Level 2, Level 3, and Seamanship Skills of the National Sailing Scheme, and Youth Sailing Scheme up to Stage 4. He can also teach Sailing with Spinnakers with the approval of the Principal and Day Sailing under the supervision of a coastal SI. The following endorsements are designed to extend the scope of an instructor's ability and will increase his value to the Principal of a training centre.

COASTAL ENDORSEMENT

Role

- Instructors and Senior Instructors wishing to operate at a coastal venue must hold a coastal award.
- Mediterranean training centres are classified as coastal.
- A coastal endorsement applies to all other instructor endorsements, including the Advanced Instructor award.

Training/Assessment

- Candidates should apply to a coastal centre or their Regional Development Officer for details of courses.
- Training/assessment will be given by an RYA Coach/Assessor either by:
- Two day training course with continuous assessment or
- 1 day assessment.
- Assessment will be based on the pre-entry skill test and sailing techniques on tidal waters.

ADVANCED INSTRUCTOR ENDORSEMENT

The Advanced Instructor (ADI) must have the background knowledge, technical ability and skills to demonstrate any of the Sailing with Spinnakers or Performance Sailing techniques. Teaching people how to sail performance boats requires a subtle change in the attitude of the instructor. There are many different skills to learn from a coaching point of view. While many people will wish to receive coaching or instruction in race standard Wayfarers or GP14s, many of the newer boats will be a lot faster, so an appropriate coaching style will be required. While students will know the basic skills required to get the boat from A to B, instructors have to be able to analyse their performance, give positive feedback and coach them progressively. ADIs must be confident in sailing the boats in which they are coaching.

There are a number of areas that the ADIs' endorsement will focus on.

Role

- An Advanced Instructor is an experienced instructor with a broad background of sailing experience.
- Has been trained to teach Performance Sailing and Sailing with Spinnakers from the RYA National Sailing Scheme.

Eligibility

- Candidates will hold the RYA Instructor certificate.
- Have at least 1 season's teaching experience.
- Possess skills to at least the Performance Sailing and Sailing with Spinnakers modules.
- Will have powerboat handling skills in a teaching environment.

Training/Assessment

- Candidates should apply to their Regional Development Officer for details of courses.
- Attend a two day training/continuous assessment course covering the following content:
- Performance boat handling, spinnaker handling, 5 essentials coaching, use of powerboats.
- The course may include a theory test.
- A certificate will be issued by the RYA upon successful completion.

DINGHY/KEELBOAT/MULTIHULL ENDORSEMENT

Role

Instructors who completed their initial training course and assessment in one boat discipline, but who subsequently want to instruct in another, should obtain these endorsements.

- Candidates should apply to their Regional Development Officer for details of courses.
- Training will be given by an authorised RYA Coach/Assessor.
- Candidates will attend a two day training/assessment course during which they will be asked to demonstrate pre-entry test skills and teaching techniques in the new discipline.
- A certificate will be issued by the RYA upon successful completion.

Eligibility

- Candidates will hold the RYA Dinghy/Keelboat/Multihull Instructor certificate.
- Have at least one season's teaching experience.
- Possess skills to at least the Seamanship and Sailing with Spinnakers modules.
- Will have powerboat handling skills in a teaching environment.

Training/Assessment

- A pre-entry assessment with appropriate modifications for each boat discipline will be included.
- Attend a 2 day training/continuous assessment course.
- The course may include a theory test.
- A certificate will be issued by the RYA upon successful completion.

RACING INSTRUCTOR ENDORSEMENT

The majority of dinghy sailing in Britain takes place in clubs; most clubs organise racing which is a main focus of their activities. Many people learn to sail each year but can be put off the sport when faced for the first time with the apparent complexities of club racing.

The Racing Instructor course is designed to enable instructors to introduce relatively inexperienced sailors to club racing. All RYA Instructor courses should include approximately half a day of practical training in the subject.

Role

This endorsement can be obtained by instructors with experience of club racing who wish to teach racing skills through the Start Racing module of the RYA sailing schemes. Racing Instructors with sufficient personal racing experience will also be permitted to teach the Intermediate and Advanced Racing courses.

Eligibility

RYA Instructors who have experience of club racing (minimum completed 9 races plus assisted race officer) may qualify during their instructor training course. Alternatively, qualified instructors may undertake further training at a later date with a Coach/Assessor.

Training/Assessment

The one day course will include the organisation of club racing, preparation and management of the Start Racing course and instructional techniques afloat including the use of race training exercises. On successful completion, a record card will be completed by an RYA Coach/Assessor and sent to the RYA. Assessment is continuous.

The course should include the following characteristics:

- An emphasis on racing as fun.
- Ensuring that starts and rules are not intimidating.
- The provision of enough information for Level 2/3 standard sailors to get round a club racing course safely, without presenting a hazard to other sailors.
- Encouragement to sailors to start racing, join a club and progress within the sport.

RACING COACH LEVEL 2

Role

A qualified RYA Racing Coach Level 2 is a good club racer with personal knowledge of club and/or regional racing and a broad basis of coaching skills. They will be able to deliver Start, Intermediate and Advanced Racing where appropriate, working at affiliated clubs or recognised training centres.

Eligibility

- Appropriate racing experience (guide = good club racer).
- Appropriate current racing knowledge (classes/pathways).
- RYA Powerboat Level 2 certificate.
- A valid RYA First Aid certificate, or another acceptable first aid qualification as detailed on the RYA website (www.rya.org.uk/go/firstaidcertificates).
- Minimum age 16. Level 2 Coaches aged under 18 should be appropriately supervised by an adult who is either a Senior Instructor or a Racing Coach Level 2 or above.
- Previous instructing experience is preferred but is not essential if the candidate has suitable alternative experience.

Training/Assessment

The course to become an RYA Racing Coach Level 2 is an intense weekend/two day course looking at the theory of coaching and applying it in a practical series of on the water exercises.

Each candidate will be expected to run complete sessions including a brief, on the water exercises with feedback and a debrief. The aim of the course is to provide candidates with skills and techniques to coach racing to youth and adult sailors. Assessment is continuous.

Revalidation

Racing Coaches are requested to revalidate every 5 years to ensure their continued effectiveness as a coach.

- Complete the Revalidation Form on the Racing Coaches section of the RYA website and send it to: Caroline Sullivan, Racing Department, RYA House, Ensign Way, Hamble, Southampton, Hants SO31 4YA

You also need to send a copy of:

- A valid First Aid certificate. To see if your first aid certificate is valid go to:

http://www.rya.org.uk/coursestraining/resources/Pages/Firstaidandmedical.aspx

RYA SENIOR INSTRUCTOR

The Principal of an RYA Training Centre carries the formal responsibility for ensuring that all training complies with RYA guidelines, laid down in the current Guidance Notes for inspection of RYA Recognised Training Centres. The Principal may himself be a Senior Instructor or may appoint a Senior Instructor to act as sailing manager, and to ensure that sailing tuition is organised according to RYA methods and standards.

The qualities required of a Senior Instructor are patience, resourcefulness, and the ability to deal with students and instructors. SIs should also have the organisational ability to ensure that courses are safe, enjoyable, and informative.

Quite apart from his responsibility to his students, the Senior Instructor has a responsibility to his instructors, to his club or employer and the RYA.

Senior Instructor training is a combination of teaching and work experience. Courses are organised on a regional basis with minimum numbers in order to bring together candidates with a variety of backgrounds and instructing experience.

The course may be split into two weekends or a number of days, with the separate sessions being run at different centres within a region. This gives candidates the opportunity of working at different places and hence being introduced to different operational problems.

Those wishing to apply for a SI course should do so to their Regional Development Officer, who will have information regarding where courses are being run in their particular region. They will group together applicants in order to ensure that the course runs. The course will only run if there are sufficient candidates to make it viable.

Once accepted, the candidate will receive the 'SI workbook'. This must be completed before attending the course as well as any preparation set by the training coaches. Failure to do so will have a direct effect on the outcome.

An RYA recognised dinghy/keelboat/multihull training centre must have a current Senior Instructor as its Principal or Chief Instructor.

Role

The SI is an experienced instructor who has been trained and assessed to be competent in the following areas:

- Organise and manage RYA National Sailing Scheme sailing courses.
- Organise and control group sailing tuition of all ages and abilities.
- Supervising, directing and assisting a team of Instructors and Assistant Instructors.

Eligibility

Candidates must first be an RYA Dinghy/Keelboat/Multihull Instructor and must fulfil the following criteria before taking part in the Senior Instructor training course:

- Minimum age 18.
- Two years intermittent or one year full time instructing since qualifying.
- RYA Safety Boat certificate.
- A valid RYA First Aid certificate, or another acceptable first aid qualification as detailed on the RYA website (www.rya.org.uk/go/firstaidcertificates).
- Signed recommendation from the Principal of an RYA Training Centre (see page 126).

During the course candidates will be asked to demonstrate that they have sailing ability to at least the standard of an RYA Instructor.

Training/Assessment

- Candidates should apply to their Regional Development Officer for details of courses.
- Courses are organised through the RDO on a regional basis and require a minimum of 6 candidates.
- Courses are staffed by two RYA Coaches/Assessors.
- The course will be four days, but can be spread over two weekends with course material sent out prior to the course.

- Assessment will be on a continual basis.
- Course content includes personal sailing, course preparation, organisation and management, feedback and debriefing skills, customer and instructor liaison, safeguarding children and vulnerable adults, centre administration.

Certificate Validity

Revalidation can be done in three ways:

- Senior Instructor certificates valid for five years from date of issue if supported by a valid first aid certificate.
- Certificates can be revalidated by obtaining and returning a completed revalidation form accompanied by a log of teaching experience in an RYA Training Centre, valid first aid certificate, valid RYA membership number or appropriate fee.
- Little or no logged experience may require a re-assessment to ensure the instructor is still up to date.
- Revalidation should normally include all existing instructor endorsements.

The SI Training Course

As the SI course may be the last formal course which most instructors attend, it aims to cover as many of their needs as possible; it is impossible to do this by didactic or dictatorial teaching.

Therefore, the course has the following format:

- A number of short on water tasks/sessions planned, led and debriefed by the candidates.
- Shore based teaching sessions.
- Candidate delivered presentations.
- Candidate led workshops/discussions.
- Training tasks led by specialist coaches.
- Continuous assessment with regular feedback after each session from the coaches running the course.
- Sessions will be allocated to candidates on any part of the syllabus encouraging fresh input to candidates' skills.

The Senior Instructor will be capable of managing and supervising one or more groups afloat, each group taught by an appropriately qualified instructor. They will also understand the full requirements of RYA Training Centre Recognition and where necessary put in place all the necessary systems and documentation. This may well include carrying out or revising a risk assessment and specifying and recording safety procedures.

Coastal Senior Instructor courses will include training in the delivery of the Day Sailing course. Careful planning, group control, appropriate safety cover and constant awareness are vital for safe day trips from coastal venues. Candidates will receive input and be expected to demonstrate these qualities during the course.

Course Organisation

The most important part of the Senior Instructor's role is day-to-day organisation of each course. Every course has four elements:

The students

The instructors

The fleet/teaching facilities

The syllabus

It is the task of the Senior Instructor to ensure that they all fit together harmoniously. Apart from those caused by deteriorating weather conditions, problems usually arise from poor planning or a lack of communication between the SI, instructors and students.

Therefore, the SI is responsible for and should consider the following:

- Correct teaching ratios.
- Correct student/instructor matching (father/son, husband/wife).

- Group control ashore and afloat.
- The 'house rules' of the centre including equipment stowage.
- Safe slipway and launching procedures.
- Safe and effective use of safety boats and their allocation.
- Ensuring all staff including visiting ones know what is expected of them.
- Students learning, content and pace of sessions.
- An awareness of weather conditions and calling a halt to on-water activities.
- Alternative teaching programme in the event of adverse weather (high/no wind).
- In the case of postponement, re-programming staff and facilities.
- The SI should have an overall awareness of what is happening on the water amongst all the fleets operating to anticipate potential problems and avoid them.

Before each practical session, the SI must be confident that each of his instructors has a clear idea of the aim and purpose of that session, so that they can confirm that the aims have been met during the debriefing.

It should already be clear that an SI has a great deal of responsibility, relying on resourcefulness to solve problems as they arise. Apart from directing the work of instructors, the SI should assist and support them, particularly when they need advice. The following summary of brief questions might provoke further thoughts. How should these be answered?

Ten Questions from Instructors

1. One of my students is learning far more quickly that the others. What do I do?
2. It's blowing Force 5 out there, what do I do?
   (Day 2 of a beginner's course).
3. What should I do with my hands when I'm lecturing?
4. You've asked me in to cover for Robin whilst he's away, how do I know what his students have covered so far? (Third day of a Seamanship course).
5. How do I tell when my students are ready to move on to the next stage of the syllabus?
6. Bob and Sally say they're too old to take part in the capsize drill. What can I tell them?
7. What do I do if three of my Toppers capsize at once?
8. Why should I shave? (From a 22-year-old male instructor.)
9. Why should I bother with the kill cord on the outboard? It only gets in the way.
10. How do I teach Jenny to sail? She's only got one hand.

Some of those questions should never arise, but instructors will always look to the SI for advice. **This should be encouraged.** Even though they should know the answers, the SI must treat questions from instructors in just the same way that they should treat questions from students. It could be considered that instructors are also the SI's customers.

Catastrophe Clinic

One of the advantages of a large Senior Instructor course is that it brings together candidates with a wide, varied collective experience of teaching sailing. One useful way of sharing that experience is by the exercise known as Catastrophe Clinic.

Each candidate writes a short outline of the worst things which have happened to them whilst teaching sailing. The outline should contain details of:

- The type of venue (inland, estuary, open sea).
- The size of fleet and type of boats.
- The number of students and the level of course.
- The number of instructors and teaching or rescue boats.
- What happened.

The group leader then collects all the examples and introduces them one by one for group discussion, with the author of each scenario remaining silent when his 'catastrophe' is discussed.

After the group has discussed the problem and decided what they would have done in the circumstances, the author then explains what he actually did and why.

Some problems may result from the unexpected behaviour of instructors or students and will call upon the SI's resources of tact and diplomacy in finding a solution.

The real epics usually result from not one single problem but a string of circumstances, each one of which on its own might not have been so serious. The horror of multiple capsizes in deteriorating weather conditions, possibly with dangerous lee shore or commercial shipping nearby, calls for clear thinking to establish priorities and act decisively. The two Golden Rules in such circumstances are:

- **Count heads**
- **Save people before property**

One recurring theme, which is not highlighted above, is that of the student with a health problem, either unknown or undisclosed. Examples range from the teenage diabetic on a residential course who forgets his medication in the excitement of the activity, to the middle aged man who suffers a suspected heart attack during a capsize recovery session and the woman who collapses in the hot shower after sailing, for reasons totally unconnected with the activity.

All have specific lessons for the Senior Instructor but the overall message is that the SI in control of the group must know of any health problems. The usual way of finding out is to require all students to complete a health declaration.

Senior Instructor Assessment

Throughout your SI course you will be assessed on your ability to plan, organise and run practical sessions, and on your input to shorebased sessions. In particular, the training coaches are looking for:

- Aims clearly stated (did the session have clear objectives?).
- Briefing was complete and clear (did the group know what was required?).
- Sailing area identified.
- Could the leader be clearly identified?
- That the whole group was involved.
- Enthusiasm was maintained.
- Problems were solved.
- Signals (two way) were established including 'Abandon'.
- On-water coaching took place.
- Group control was maintained (no unnecessary delays) ashore and afloat.
- Each student was carefully debriefed and problems discussed and solved.
- Session achieved all objectives.
- Students' questions were answered.
- Students were informed of their successes. The follow-on session was described.
- The equipment was carefully put away after the session.

Good Relationships with Others

In addition, the training coaches will be applying an assessment based on their experience of the RYA Coaching Scheme to decide whether the candidate meets the requirements of a Senior Instructor. If they are unable to confirm that they have successfully completed the course, the Coaches will outline the reasons for that decision and an action plan will be set for future success.

RYA COACH/ASSESSOR

An RYA Coach/Assessor is an experienced Senior Instructor with an Advanced Instructor Endorsement who has been trained and assessed as competent to themselves train and assess Instructors and Senior Instructors, and appointed to deliver such training by the RYA Chief Instructor. Coaches/Assessors are appointed on an annual basis, and attend an update every five years.

Eligibility

A Senior Instructor with proven ability and extensive experience of the National Sailing Scheme and Youth Sailing Scheme in a variety of training centres. These qualities are expected to include a thoroughly competent level of personal sailing ability, good teaching, motivating and leadership skills, good fleet management, excellent coaching skills and a positive enthusiastic approach based on good communication skills.

A mature approach is necessary. Training candidate instructors can be a challenging business, demanding delicate judgement.

Regional Development Officers and Regional Coaches nominate potential Coaches/Assessors to the RYA Chief Instructor.

Coaches/Assessors based overseas are occasionally trained where a requirement can be demonstrated. In this case the first approach should be to the RYA HQ.

It is a requirement to be an RYA member on application and for the duration of your appointment.

Preparation/Selection (2 days)

Candidates should be able to:
- Demonstrate and teach any part of the National Sailing Scheme including all the modules.
- Sail competently in a variety of boats including single handers and high performance craft.
- Plan and manage a course involving sessions ashore and afloat.
- Demonstrate effective safety boat and coach boat skills.
- Give a formal presentation including the use of visual aids, and chair a discussion.
- Show enthusiasm, motivation and leadership.

Training Course

The five-day training course will include:
- The skills of teaching and assessing RYA Instructors.
- The RYA National Sailing Scheme and Youth Sailing Scheme and standards required for instructional awards.
- Administration of the scheme.
- Advanced seamanship techniques.
- High performance sailing.
- Techniques of Senior Instructor training.
- Teaching students with special needs, safeguarding and child protection.

Coach/Assessor Updating

After five years Coaches/Assessors must attend a short practical updating course organised by the RYA. The update will include:
- Techniques for teaching and assessing instructors.
- Information on changes to the schemes.
- An opportunity to feed back to the RYA.
- Practical sailing and coaching.
- Peer to peer review.

Apprenticeship

Candidates who complete the training course successfully will normally be expected to organise and run their first instructor course with the help and mentoring of a more experienced Coach/Assessor. On successful completion of this they will be appointed as an RYA Coach/Assessor.

Coaches/Assessors wishing to train Instructors in other boat disciplines such as keelboat or multihull should normally have suitable experience and/or the relevant instructor endorsement.

Coaches/Assessors wishing to become RYA Training Centre Inspectors should attend a one-day training course organised by the RYA.

WHO TEACHES WHAT IN THE RYA NATIONAL SAILING SCHEME AND YOUTH SAILING SCHEME

	National Sailing Scheme in dinghies	National Sailing Scheme in keelboats	National Sailing Scheme in multihulls	Youth Sailing Scheme
Dinghy Instructor	Levels 1, 2, 3, Day Sailing, Seamanship Skills, Sailing with Spinnakers*			Stages 1, 2, 3, 4 in dinghies
Keelboat Instructor		Levels 1, 2, 3, Day Sailing, Seamanship Skills, Sailing with Spinnakers*		Stages 1, 2, 3, 4 in keelboats
Multihull Instructor			Levels 1, 2, 3, Day Sailing, Seamanship Skills, Sailing with Spinnakers*	Stages 1, 2, 3, 4 in multihulls
Advanced Instructor	As Dinghy Instructor plus Sailing with Spinnakers, Performance Sailing	As Keelboat Instructor plus Sailing with Spinnakers and Performance Sailing	As Multihull Instructor plus Sailing with Spinnakers and Performance Sailing	As Dinghy Instructor plus Sailing with Spinnakers, Performance Sailing
Senior Instructor	As Dinghy Instructor plus Sailing with Spinnakers	As Keelboat instructor plus Sailing with Spinnakers	As Multihull Instructor plus Sailing with Spinnakers	As Dinghy Instructor plus Sailing with Spinnakers
Racing Instructor/ Racing Coach Level 1	As Dinghy Instructor plus Start Racing, Intermediate Racing,* Advanced Racing*	As Keelboat Instructor plus Start Racing, Intermediate Racing,* Advanced Racing*	As Multihull Instructor plus Start Racing, Intermediate Racing,* Advanced Racing*	As Dinghy Instructor plus Start Racing, Intermediate Racing,* Advanced Racing*
Racing Coach Level 2	Start Racing, Intermediate Racing, Advanced Racing	Start Racing, Intermediate Racing, Advanced Racing	Start Racing, Intermediate Racing, Advanced Racing	Start Racing, Intermediate Racing, Advanced Racing
Racing Coach Level 3	Start Racing, Intermediate Racing, Advanced Racing	Start Racing, Intermediate Racing, Advanced Racing	Start Racing, Intermediate Racing, Advanced Racing	Start Racing, Intermediate Racing, Advanced Racing
RYA Coach/ Assessor	All NSS and YSS courses plus Dinghy Instructor/ SI Courses and endorsements	All NSS and YSS courses plus Keelboat Instructor/ SI Courses and endorsements	All NSS and YSS courses plus Multihull Instructor/ SI Courses and endorsements	All NSS and YSS courses plus Dinghy Instructor/ SI Courses and endorsements

*Instructor who is suitably experienced and approved by the Principal or Chief Instructor.
A dinghy Senior Instructor holding RYA Day Skipper Practical or above may teach and supervise the NSS in keelboats.
N.B. All RYA tuition should be supervised by an RYA Senior Instructor.

TEACHING RATIOS WITHIN THE NATIONAL SAILING SCHEME/ YOUTH SAILING SCHEME

TYPE OF CRAFT	STUDENT:INSTRUCTOR RATIO
Crewed dinghies and multihulls	3:1 for beginners with instructor onboard Maximum 9:1 but not more than 6 boats per instructor (e.g. 3 Wayfarers with 3 students in each, or 4 Picos with 2 students in each)
Single handed dinghies and multihulls	6:1 (applies only whilst the boats are used as single handers)
Keelboats	Day boats/keelboats without accommodation: 4:1 (instructor on board) 1 instructor must be responsible for no more than 9 students (e.g. 3 boats with 3 students in each)

TEACHING RATIOS FOR INSTRUCTOR TRAINING COURSES

DELIVERED BY	COURSE	Ratio	Moderated
Senior Instructor	Assistant Instructor	1:6	NO
Coach Assessor	Dinghy Instructor	1:6	YES
Coach Assessor	Keelboat Instructor*	1:6	YES
Coach Assessor	Multihull Instructor*	1:6	YES
Coach Assessor	Dinghy Instructor Endorsement	1:6	YES
Coach Assessor	Keelboat Instructor Endorsement*	1:6	NO
Coach Assessor	Multihull Instructor Endorsement*	1:6	NO
Coach Assessor	Coastal Endorsement	1:6	NO
Coach Assessor	Advanced Instructor Endorsement	1:6	NO
Coach Assessor	Racing Instructor Endorsement/Racing Coach L1	1:6	NO
Coach Assessor	Senior Instructor	Min. 6 candidates	YES Throughout course
Racing Coach Tutor	Racing Coach Level 2	Max. 6 candidates	NO
Coaching Development Manager	Racing Coach Level 3	Max. 12 candidates	YES Throughout course
Coaching Development Manager	Racing Coach Tutor	Individual assessment	NO

*Coach/Assessor approved by RYA Chief Instructor.

6 Techniques for Instructing and Coaching

INSTRUCTING AND COACHING SKILLS

As an RYA Instructor you will deliver teaching material as both an instructor and coach. Which one it is will depend on a number of factors:

- The type of session (practical or theory).
- The subject (new subject or developing existing techniques and skills).
- The teaching method (discussion, demonstration or student practise).
- The environment (ashore or afloat).
- Number of students.
- Where they are in the RYA scheme.

Your role as an instructor is to help students learn through teaching them practical and theoretical aspects of the sport. It mostly involves explaining and demonstrating techniques that are new to them.

However, coaching implies a shift towards helping students develop those techniques into skills. It might involve more observation, feedback and questioning to check their understanding of the skills.

A typical session might follow this simple structure:

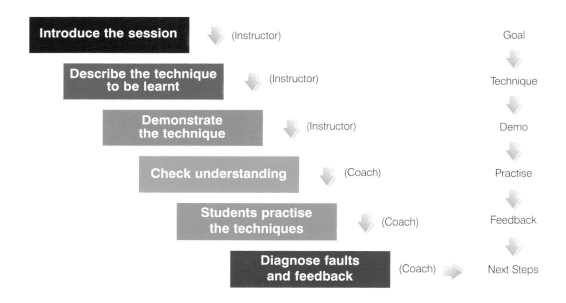

Introduce the session	(Instructor)	Goal
Describe the technique to be learnt	(Instructor)	Technique
Demonstrate the technique	(Instructor)	Demo
Check understanding	(Coach)	Practise
Students practise the techniques	(Coach)	Feedback
Diagnose faults and feedback	(Coach)	Next Steps

This simple model shows how your role evolves from instructor to coach as your students progress through their course.

If you coach your students effectively their performance should improve and any problems that prevent them progressing can be solved.

Effective Coaching Needs:

- A mutual desire to coach/be coached.
- Empathy towards your students.
- Good communication between coach and student.
- A focus on clear achievable goals.

There are three main processes involved in coaching:

Communication:
Listening, questioning, responding and giving feedback

Influencing:
Increasing confidence and independence in your students

Positively reinforcing things done well

Helping:
Expressing concern for, and empathy with, their development

Establishing support for your students

Identifying students' needs and linking this to their goals

Remember that we are communicating all the time. Our thoughts and emotions can often 'leak' out through our verbal and non-verbal communication.

Coaches should therefore:
Develop their verbal and non-verbal communication skills

Ensure that they provide positive feedback during sessions

Give all students equal or appropriate attention

Ensure that they listen to their students, not just talk!

Helping your Students to Learn

Sailing is a fun, practical and exciting sport which requires experiential learning – in other words **learning through doing**. It helps to break it down into four stages. In simple terms this means:

- Run a structured activity or session.
- Review and discuss what happened during the session.
- Help your students learn and be sure about what they know.
- Encourage students to apply their learning to future sessions.

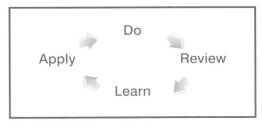

Throughout this process students need:

- Positive and constructive feedback.
- Time to reflect.
- Structured sessions that build on each other.

Exactly how you tackle these four stages can be determined by understanding how your students absorb information and learn new skills.

Absorbing Information

Not everyone sees and experiences the world in the same way. We take in information through our senses:
- Visual – eyes.
- Auditory – ears.
- Kinaesthetic – touch, feel and movement.

These senses are pathways to our brains. None of us use one pathway exclusively – there is significant overlap between them, but your students are likely to have a preference:

Visual Learners

They like:
- Written information.
- Pictures and observation.
- Sessions that have a lot of content to observe i.e. demonstrations and visual aids.

Auditory Learners

They like:
- Information contained in the spoken word.
- Clear verbal explanations/briefings.
- Verbal feedback.
- Discussions.

Top Tip

What I hear, I forget
What I see, I remember
What I do, I understand

Kinaesthetic Learners

They like:
- Learning through touch and movement.
- To 'have a go' and see what happens.

So, by adapting your teaching style to suit these three preferences, you should be able to create a learning environment with something for everyone.

Once we have absorbed information, we need to process it in order for us to learn. In the same way that we have a preference for absorbing information, we also tend to have a preference for how we learn from this information. Just as people have a tendency towards left or right handedness, which influences how they tackle manual tasks, many people have a particular learning style which influences how they approach mental tasks.

As instructors or coaches, by being aware of different learning preferences or styles we are able to modify our own teaching style to suit that of our students.

Tips for Reinforcing Learning

- Always put new techniques into context – understanding is helped if you see the 'big picture'.
- The average person can deal with approximately seven chunks of information – don't overload them.
- People remember the beginning and end, but often miss the middle – keep demonstrations and explanations short and structured.
- Keep information memorable – use unusual, funny or unexpected ways to illustrate your teaching.
- Use a range of methods to teach important skills in order to cater for your students' range of learning styles – i.e. explaining, showing a video, visualizing, reading, looking at pictures etc.
- Ensure that new skills become well-established with plenty of practice and reinforcement.
- Focus your students on what they should do, rather than what they should not do, or they might end up doing the very opposite to what they should!

Demonstrations are particularly important and useful in sailing, so demonstrate whenever possible. People will need time to identify what is being taught, so link the parts into a smooth skill that becomes automatic.

This leads us to the 'whole – part – whole' demonstration method, where the skill is executed at normal speed, then broken into detailed parts, then redone at normal speed. In this way both a mental picture and a detailed understanding can be conveyed.

Use of Land Drills

It is possible to teach the entire syllabus without ever using any land drills, providing a number of factors are present. These are, good/perfect sailing conditions which include the venue, a dinghy that the student(s) are comfortable in, receptive student(s) able to act immediately and consistently on input and effective communication between student(s) and instructor.

Only one of these elements needs to be missing to 'break the chain', therefore instructors should consider using land drills where they will enhance/accelerate or reinforce student learning.

LAND DRILLS

- Land drills introduce clarity and simplicity. They enable students to achieve more in less time afloat. They are not an end in themselves, nor are they always necessary or appropriate.
- Land drills work particularly well after a demonstration afloat to convey the 'big picture'.
- Introduce the session by explaining why the land drill may be useful.
- Make it as real as possible. Boats are much better than ropes and chairs.
- If using a boat, make sure it is safe on its trolley with people aboard, or put it on grass or even in the water.
- Position the students where they can see clearly but are safe. Be aware of any distractions.
- What you do is more important than what you say. Use few words and demonstrate smoothly at normal speed, before breaking the manoeuvre down.
- Most instructors talk too much as they demonstrate.
- Involve your students where possible e.g. in moving the boom or balancing the boat.
- When teaching children, consider increasing entertainment by turning the drill into play by the use of songs or other ideas.
- Land drills are useful for a number of skills e.g. spinnaker work, anchoring, reefing etc., where a complicated series of actions have to be co-ordinated.

THE FOUR STAGES OF LEARNING – UNCONSCIOUS INCOMPETENCE TO UNCONSCIOUS COMPETENCE

You can expect your students largely to follow the same stages when learning any new technique. Indeed, as they progress up through the stages with one technique they may begin again at the bottom with new techniques or skills.

Four Stages of Competence

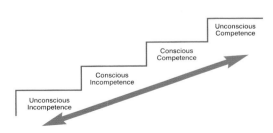

Unconscious Incompetence
Students don't know what they don't know.

Conscious Incompetence
Students are aware of what they don't know. For some this adds clarity, others find it daunting and frustrating.

Conscious Competence
Students are becoming competent but still have to think about what they are doing and how they do it. Following simple sequences will be useful at this stage.

Unconscious Competence
Students now do things with very little conscious thought. Things flow and are effortless.

Basic Skills Model

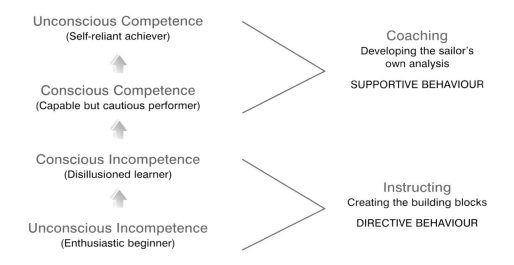

Unconscious Competence
(Self-reliant achiever)

Conscious Competence
(Capable but cautious performer)

Conscious Incompetence
(Disillusioned learner)

Unconscious Incompetence
(Enthusiastic beginner)

Coaching
Developing the sailor's
own analysis

SUPPORTIVE BEHAVIOUR

Instructing
Creating the building blocks

DIRECTIVE BEHAVIOUR

Instructors should adapt their approach as students develop competence and become more skilful, initially instructing and being directive in their approach to the development of good technique but eventually becoming less directive and more supportive as technique becomes more skilful and adopting a more coaching role.

HOW AND WHY PEOPLE LEARN

Adults and young people often learn in different ways and for different reasons:

THE WAY ADULTS LEARN	TIPS TO HELP
Typically more independent and self directed	Once given a task, they will get on with it and will not need 'watching' to complete it. Sometimes can be difficult to get them to stop.
Goal orientated and structured approach to learning. They have become used to being lectured. They can find the relaxed RYA session uncomfortable	Encourage them to answer questions and to question the content of the session in general. Don't allow anyone to opt out.
Need to know why they are learning something	Ensure that the purpose as well as the aim of the session is made clear at the start.
Accumulated life experience can be applied to the learning process for good and bad. They are also used to 'problem solving'	Use this to advantage and incorporate it into sessions. It may make sessions longer, however.
Often reluctant to get things wrong and appear foolish, especially in front of the group and become frustrated when they do!	Reward correct answers/solutions and encourage those who answer incorrectly to find the right ones.

THE WAY CHILDREN LEARN	TIPS TO HELP
More random and instructor/coach led	Providing they are occupied and interested, they will respond to teaching input.
Fun and experiential orientated approach	This doesn't include classrooms! Motivation can dip if too long is spent in one. Explore alternatives, work cards, models, constructive games, allow students to draw their understanding on the white board.
Need to know why they are learning something	Ensure that the purpose as well as the aim of the session is made clear at the start.
Want to know 'what', 'where' and 'when' rather than 'why'	They are much more 'active' in their learning.
May be experiencing the skill for the first time. Not biased by other experiences, they're free learners	Often, young people make better students. They can learn faster and have better powers of retention.
A more natural approach with fewer inhibitions. Happy to get things wrong!	Don't expect perfection in the sessions.
Youngsters can be shy and reluctant to participate, especially if they have few or no friends in the group	Involve them with simple questions and enthusiastically reward correct answers. Check understanding with a 'fun' quiz.
Enthusiasm can lead to boisterous behaviour and even loss of control. Be vigilant of this	Ensure that the youngsters know 'who is in charge' and check unruly behaviour early. A simple way to stop idle chatter is to sit the group down.
Use the Youth Sailing Scheme	It has advice on different approaches and learning styles.

People often learn best through fun and enjoyment. Make your sessions fun and stimulating for all.

What Might Motivate our Students to Learn?

• Making or maintaining social relationships.

• Learning to engage others – parents often learn with a view to involving the rest of their family.

• A desire to achieve awards and qualifications.

• Escape or stimulation from everyday life.

• Interest in the subject.

•Lifestyle aspiration.

• Fear of failure.

Being aware of your students' possible motivations for taking the course helps you to shape it, the materials you use and how you structure the groups in which they are placed for teaching.

BARRIERS TO LEARNING

- Other responsibilities (families, careers, social commitments).
- Lack of time.
- Environment – being wet and cold!
- Feelings – looking or feeling silly.
- Scheduling problems – when courses take place.
- Insufficient confidence.
- Inappropriate teaching methods.
- Culture clash – young fit blond instructor vs. unfit, middle-aged student.
- Personality clashes – between student and instructor.
- Having to learn, if told by parent or spouse but not interested or ready.
- Fear of failure (again).

WELL, LITTLE BEN AINSLIE WAS **BEGGING** FOR MY ADVICE.

Fear

Fear is one of the main barriers which you, a good instructor, can help the students overcome.

Adults and children normally have three principal fears when trying something for the first time:

Fear of failure – Be clear about their progress throughout the course. Encourage them to try things out, even if it means making mistakes. If the course is assessed, let your students know the outcome.

Fear of the unknown – Keep your students fully informed throughout the course, the stages they will go through and why you are structuring the course that way.

Fear of not being liked or fitting in – Break the ice early and encourage groups to work together and get to know each other. Consider some games to help people relax.

PEOPLE SKILLS FOR INSTRUCTORS

What your Students Think of You

How you are perceived by others determines your credibility and therefore the influence you will have over them. First impressions are vital as it is estimated that up to 90% of people's opinions of you are formed in the first four minutes of meeting you. Therefore, you will start with a disadvantage if your students arrive for the course only to find you stressed and bedraggled, trying to open up the centre, tidy up the mess left by the previous group, getting equipment stores open and rescue boats afloat.

Tips for gaining your students' trust:

- The first four minutes of any encounter are the most important and set the scene.
- Always set up early and be ready for their arrival.
- Pay attention to your personal appearance and grooming as this can exert an inordinate influence on their first impression of you.
- Listen to your students and respect what they tell you – the more you listen, the more you can influence them.
- Spend time with them to enable a rapport to develop.

What you Need to Know about your Students

Remember that amongst your students you are going to have widely differing ages, genders, backgrounds, skills, hopes, fears, expectations and aspirations.

It's a good idea to gather as much information as possible on these areas from your students prior to the course. Some of this can be done on booking forms or simple questionnaires. Questions you might want to ask of beginners:

- Why do you want to learn to sail?
- Have you done any sailing before, when, where etc?
- Do you take part in any other water sports?
- What will you do once you are able to sail?

…and so on.

Being prepared with this information can help you to:

- Create the right environment.
- Be warm, welcoming and friendly.
- Tell them a bit about yourself.
- Get them all talking about themselves.
- Tell them what to expect (and what not to expect).
- 'Create the course' (together).
- Break the ice.

COMMUNICATION SKILLS

Communication is more than just words. We are constantly communicating, even when we are saying nothing.

Research has shown that 55% of your communication is determined by your body language, posture and eye contact, 38% by your tone of voice, and only 7% by your actual words. Therefore, to get your message across, concentrate on how you talk, not just what you say.

Whatever you say, typically your students will:

- Filter: Pick out more or less important bits for themselves.
- Distort: Interpret things for themselves.
- Delete: Remove any bits that they find unclear or too difficult.

Remember that often **less is more** – keep your messages simple and free of jargon, and back them up with demonstrations and practical examples.

Check your students' understanding of new information as often as possible, using open questions to enable them to confirm what you have said or what you want them to do.

Remember the worst question in the world is…'Do you understand?' There will only ever be one answer – 'yes'.

Non-verbal Messages

People use a variety of behaviour to maintain a smooth flow of communication, such as head-nods, smiles, frowns, laughter etc. Your students' facial expressions provide you with some feedback on the session. Glazed or down-turned eyes indicate boredom or disinterest, as does fidgeting. Fully raised eyebrows signal disbelief and half raised indicate puzzlement. The posture of the group enables you to judge their attitude and mood.

Communication Blocks

Communication difficulties between the instructor and the student can happen for a number of reasons:

- The student's perception of something is not the same as yours.
- The student may jump to a conclusion instead of working through the process of hearing, understanding and accepting.
- The student may lack the knowledge and understanding of what you are trying to teach.
- The student may lack the motivation.
- The instructor may have difficulty in expressing what they want to say.
- Emotions may interfere in the communication process.
- There may be a clash of personalities.

Effective Communication

Effective communication contains six elements:

- **CLEAR**   Ensure that the information is presented clearly.
- **CONCISE**   Be concise: do not lose the message by being long winded.
- **CORRECT**   Be accurate, avoid giving misleading information.
- **COMPLETE**   Give all the information and not just part of it.
- **COURTEOUS**   Be polite and non-threatening, avoid conflict.
- **CONSTRUCTIVE**   Be positive, avoid being critical and negative.

Always check that:

- You have your students' attention.
- Your students are accepting what you are saying.
- You are giving clear explanations and demonstrations.
- Your students have understood.

Always consider:

- WHY you need to communicate.
- WHO you are communicating with.
- WHERE and WHEN the message will best be delivered.
- WHAT you will be explaining or demonstrating.
- HOW you will get the information across.

STUDENTS DON'T LIKE BEING 'TICKED OFF' ...

Communication whilst afloat is particularly important but often goes wrong, so remember:

- Keep verbal communication to a minimum.
- Project your voice towards your students – it gets lost in the wind.
- Never shout – it implies that you are angry.
- Position your students where they can hear you best.
- Call students to you frequently for feedback and further instructions (single handers).
- Use pre-agreed visual signals.
- Use an agreed signal to confirm understanding.

Presentation Skills

It is normal for inexperienced instructors to be nervous about giving presentations, despite the fact that they know their subject matter well but, with the right frame of mind and a bit of practice, the nerves will soon start to disappear.

The fear often revolves around things going wrong, such as:

- I'll dry up.
- No one will be interested.
- I'll be boring.
- They won't like me.

- I don't know enough about my subject.
- They'll ask me difficult questions.
- I'll make a fool of myself.

However, being aware of these fears can help you to ensure that they don't come true.

Good Presentations Depend on Several Elements:

The Content

Write down what you know about the subject onto a large sheet of paper in the form of headings. If you can, try to group related things together. Even subjects which may not initially seem relevant to the presentation may help identify other things which are. Keeping your objectives in mind, sort out the relevant material using the need to know and nice to know group. Keep the 'need to know' and discard the 'nice to know' for now. Group the 'need to know' under three structured headings – a) introduction, b) main body, and c) summary and close.

- Consider the time available for the presentation. After all the 'need to know' have been included can any of the 'nice to knows' be added in? If so, choose the most relevant first.
- Group the points you have decided to include under subject headings but do not consider the sequence at this stage.
- Place the subject headings in a logical, interesting order.
- Put a time allocation on each subject and the use of each visual aid.
- Make working notes for the presentation.

The Words

- Clear, concise, jargon-free language.
- Think before you speak – don't 'think out loud'!
- Emphasise the important bits.
- Summarise what you've said and ask questions.

How You Say Them

- Vary your voice tone and pitch.
- Vary the pace.
- Speak in a conversational way.
- If you speak quickly build in pauses.
- Project your voice.
- Use silences – pause before important points.
- Don't fade at the end of sentences.

How you Look while Saying Them

- Good posture – stand tall, shoulders back.
- Make eye contact with all of the audience.
- Standing or sitting – decide which is best for you.
- Keep your head up.
- Avoid distracting mannerisms – get a friend to tell you if you have any.
- Dress to help your credibility – you can be smart and casual!
- Stop to breathe, look, listen, speak.

Structuring Presentations – Beginning, Middle and End

- Do not start talking until you are fully in position and ready.
- An early smile helps to relax both you and them.
- Rehearse your presentation, and modify as necessary.
- Have a plan 'B'.

The Beginning

Prepare an introduction that will attract your audience's attention. Tell them:

- Whether you will be giving them a handout or should they make their own notes, what you plan to cover and your structure (give headings).
- How long you will take.
- When they can ask questions.

If you are nervous, know your first few sentences off by heart and never apologise for your knowledge or speaking ability. Be relaxed and conversational.

Some possible ways of opening are:

- Ask a question that requires a show of hands.
- Begin with a quotation or tell a story.
- Ask the audience to do something.
- Describe a true (or imaginary) situation.
- State a significant and challenging statistic.
- Challenge the audience.
- Tell a joke (but only if you are really good at this).

The opening few moments of a presentation are very important. You want the audience to sit up and think 'this is going to be stimulating and important'.

The Middle

After you have grabbed your audience's attention with your introduction, move on to the bulk of your presentation, or 'the middle' .

Remember that attention wanders and your audience will pay most attention at the beginning and end of sections, so keep them short with clear headings and summaries.

The End

- Summarise your key points.
- Emphasise your themes.
- Make it significant.
- Do not end with something like 'that's about all I have to say so I'll end now'.
- Always stop before your audience want you to.
- Link back to your opening. For instance, 'When I started I said I would...'. And perhaps go through a check list of points in your intro.

Some ways of ending are:

- Issue a challenge (a gentle one).
- Appeal for action.
- Raise a laugh and tell a final anecdote.
- Point to the future.
- Finish with a quotation.
- Ask questions about what you've said.

Be aware of, but not too self-conscious of, your body movements:

Posture	Sit or stand up straight – but not rigid.
Hands	Don't be afraid of using them – as long as they are not distracting the audience.
Movement	It is fine to move about as long as, once more, this does not become a distraction.
Position	Avoid obstructions to the audiences' view of you.
View of your visual aids	Never turn your back on the audience – they won't hear you.
Eyes	Maintain eye contact with the whole audience.
Notes	Do not talk to your notes or visual aids.

HANDLING QUESTIONS

Set the Rules for Questions

Set rules for questions in the beginning i.e. save questions for the end, or ask questions whenever you like (which might be more common and useful in an informal environment). Remember, you are the leader, so lead. Whichever rule you set, make sure it's followed. Reserve the right to stop taking questions in order to ensure you have sufficient time to cover all subjects.

What to Say when you don't Know the Answer

Honesty is the only policy when presenting to a group, but blatantly admitting 'I don't know' in response to a direct question can be disastrous. No one can know the answer to every question, but it's how the situation is handled that separates great presenters from amateurs.

Don't get lulled into thinking you have seen and heard it all on a particular topic. At any time someone can come out of left field with a question you have never thought of before.

The following strategies can help you field even the toughest questions with confidence.

Reflection

Repeat the question and toss it back to your audience. 'Does anyone here have any experience with that?' The audience can save you without ever realising it. In fact, they will love to be involved and share their knowledge. After you have fielded their contributions, summarise and add your own ideas.

'I don't know the answer to that but I will find out for you.'

This is an old standard and it works well. It is an opportunity to go the extra mile, expand your knowledge, and impress your audience.

Defer to the Expert

This is a more sophisticated version of the 'Reflection' technique. Sometimes a question is legitimately outside of your area of expertise but there may be someone more experienced within the school or centre who you can pass it on to. You will need to decide who presents the answer – you or them.

Compliment the Questioner

For this to be effective, the compliment must be sincere. 'That's a good question. I've never thought about it that way. Does anyone here have any ideas on that?' You might also combine this technique with 'I'll Get Back to You'.

Use of Visual Aids

Skilful use of visual aids can greatly enhance your presentation, but don't let them take over. Always remember that your relationship with your audience is key and visual aids are just there to support you. They can take the attention off you periodically and allow you to think ahead.

Some General Tips:

• The best visual aid is a live example of your subject matter i.e. a dinghy, a buoyancy aid, a safety pack, etc. Use it as often as you can.

• If the visual is too comprehensive, your audience will switch off from you and read the visual instead.

• Whenever possible use pictures, diagrams, graphs and colour rather than lots of writing.

• Do not use too many different visual aids as you can end up in a terrible muddle.

White Boards/Blackboards

• The most common form of visual aid.

• Avoid light coloured pens as they are difficult to see at the back of the room.

• Make sure your pens have ink in them!

• Practise writing in large letters.

• Practise drawing diagrams.

• Why not use a mobile camera phone to capture the details before rubbing it off, then email it to the students if necessary?

Flip Charts

• Work well for interaction.

• Can be prepared in advance.

• Test your pens on the back of a sheet beforehand.

• Write a note for yourself in faint pencil (audience won't see).

• Bluetack up key sheets on the wall if appropriate.

• Pre draw any diagrams in faint pencil, too. Then when the time comes, overdraw them with a marker pen.

Data Projectors

- PowerPoint: good for large, formal presentations.
- Useful for key words, images and video.
- Professional effect.
- Easy to update.
- Practise well beforehand.
- Avoid too many effects and sounds!

DVDs

- Must be relevant and up to date.
- Use of video cameras for filming your students and playing footage of their own performance can be very powerful.
- Do not dwell on students' mistakes, no matter how funny.
- Use very sparingly.

Models

- Useful for highlighting specific topics.
- Easy to carry and set up.
- Students can get involved easily.
- Usually very 'low tech'.
- Especially good for showing rules of the road and racing rules.

The 'Real Thing'

- Better than just about anything else.
- Illustrates the point perfectly.
- Students can get 'hands on'.
- Saves making diagrams, drawings etc.

Whichever Method you use, Avoid:

- Too many words.
- Too much detail.
- Overcrowded slides.
- Bland images.
- Talking to the visual.
- Leaving the visual on display when you have finished with the subject matter.

Making your Visual Aids Accessible

Every individual has a different perception of what they see and read. The shape and size of words can appear different to each reader. This is especially true when working with young people and students with dyslexia. Consider that 10% of your clients may be dyslexic. Remember that changes you make to accommodate dyslexic people are good practice for everyone.

Adopting some simple strategies can help everyone to get the most from reading written information.

Font Style

- Fonts should be rounded with space between letters and reflect ordinary writing. Fonts such as Arial or Comic Sans are good.
- Where possible use lower case letters rather than capitals. Using capital letters for emphasis can make text harder to read.

Paper

- Avoid light text on a dark background.
- Use coloured paper instead of white. Cream or off-white provides a good alternative.
- Matt paper is preferable to glossy paper, as this reduces glare.
- Ensure the paper is heavy enough to prevent text showing through from the back.

Presentation Style

- Limit lines to 60 to 70 characters to avoid putting strain on the eyes.
- Use short paragraphs with space between each line and paragraph.
- Use wide margins and headings.
- Use boxes for emphasising important text.
- Use bold to highlight words rather than italics or underlining.
- Keep lines left justified with a ragged right edge.
- Use bulleted or numbered lists.
- Use this page as a guide.

Writing Style

- Write in short simple sentences.
- Be conscious of where sentences begin on the page. Starting a new sentence at the end of a line makes it harder to follow.
- Try to call the readers 'you': imagine they are sitting opposite you and you are talking to them directly.
- Give instructions clearly. Avoid long explanations.
- Stop and think before you start writing so you are clear about what you want to say.
- Use short words where possible.
- Keep your sentences to an average of 15 to 20 words.
- Be concise.

Using Flipcharts

- Keep essential information grouped together.
- Print lower case rather than using joined writing.
- Write large, it's easier for you and easier to read.
- Flow charts or models are ideal for explaining procedures.
- Use pictures and diagrams.
- List 'do's' and 'don'ts' rather than continuous text.
- Use small chunks of information, and plenty of white space, to improve readability.
- Use plain, simple and jargon-free language.
- Avoid red, orange or green as they can be hard to read for some people such as those with dyslexia.

BRIEFING AND DEBRIEFING

Sailing instructors are fortunate in that if they are teaching in double handed boats, they can instantly begin teaching their students as soon as they move to the dinghy. This will continue when they go afloat. However, teaching single handers will require a different approach as the majority of teaching input will have to be given ashore, after which the students will go afloat to try the exercise and then practise the skill.

Teaching and coaching becomes instantly more difficult when it moves to the water, but the prudent instructor will allow for this by using efficient briefing before the task and effective debriefing or feedback afterwards. This will take the place of the immediate teaching input that has been taking place ashore up to that point.

Without both of these elements, learning will only happen either by accident, or if the student is already able to analyse their own performance and then subsequently modify it.

Brief

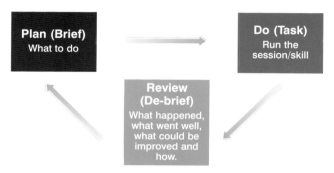

Plan (Brief)
What to do

Do (Task)
Run the session/skill

Review (De-brief)
What happened, what went well, what could be improved and how.

This should occur before every on-water session and before every new skill is introduced. Be careful though, because if it's too long, the students will switch off, becoming disinterested and perhaps miss a vital piece of information which may have a bearing on their performance or safety.

The briefing should include:

• The task; what the students should be doing.

• How to achieve the task with an explanation and demonstration if required.

• The duration of the task.

• The sailing area including the boundaries, how they will be marked and any hazards to be aware of (more relevant to single handers).

• How and where feedback will take place, if any (single handers).

• What to do if the students go out of the area (single handers).

• What the students should do in an emergency.

• What signals are to be used (including general recall and abandon session).

Once this has been given, it's only of real use if it's been understood by the students.

Please don't fall into the trap of checking understanding by asking the classic wrong question of 'Does everyone understand?' because there will only ever be one answer – 'yes!'

Instead, ask questions that relate directly to the information that's just been given,

'Where are we going to sail?' (single handers)

'What technique or task are we going to perform?'

'Which way will the dinghy turn?'

'How will you make it turn?'

'What signal will I use to bring everyone back to the beach at the end?' (single handers)

If the correct answers are coming back, then it's likely that an efficient brief has been given.

The classic 'give away' sign is when you move away to start the task, the students get into a huddle and ask themselves 'What do we do, what did the instructor say?'

The Task

The task must be chosen to suit the ability of the student. Part of the skill of instructing is to assess the student's ability and provide tuition at a challenging but not impossible level. It is very frustrating for someone with a natural flair or with some experience to be taught at the pace of the slowest beginner.

Once the task has been set, allow the student to feel responsible for it. Do not continually interrupt – if you have briefed well it should be unnecessary. If events start to go wrong a quiet word will allow the student to correct the mistake while still being in control. Never elbow students out of the way to demonstrate your skill: the idea is that they demonstrate theirs.

Occasionally, if you can, allow a mistake to be made to illustrate a point, but only do this if you feel it does not compromise safety and it is a good learning opportunity.

Debrief

Good instructing and coaching allows for students to learn in a variety of ways and is one important element of the instructor's repertoire, but providing good feedback during a debrief will always help the student understand more and maximise that learning.

Indeed, giving effective feedback is often said to be the one skill that separates the average instructor from the very good instructor.

Feedback, to be most efficient, should happen as soon after the event as possible. This implies that it should happen on the water as the student is performing the skill, or just afterwards. If this is possible, then that's where it should happen. However, for many reasons, it probably won't. So it should take place on land once the group are all safely ashore, the kit has been made safe and the students are receptive. This may mean moving to a sheltered spot, getting warmed up/cooled down, having a hot/cold drink and 'paying a visit'. It needs to be more sophisticated than a collective 'Well done, that was great, how does everyone feel?'

Each student ought to be provided with information on what they have achieved, what went well, what didn't go so well and how to put right areas that need improvement.

Any feedback methods will need some common elements to be in place beforehand and they are:

• Be clear of what the task is and know how to perform it.
• Ensure that it is achievable by the students.
• Observe the session/skill carefully.
• Record what has taken place with either a good memory or notes, if necessary.
• The instructor always remains in charge of the session, and hence safety, throughout.

Two popular feedback models being used are 'hamburger' or 'traffic light'.

The 'Hamburger', 'Sandwich' or 'Layer Cake'

It's tried and tested but has been around for a long time now. Also, the students eventually recognise the pattern.

The top. Give praise for aspects that have gone well. Be specific

The filling. What's not gone well and how to correct it. Be specific and use the 'rule of 3'. i.e. three key things which at this stage will lead to improvement

The bottom. More praise, finishing on a positive note

The 'Traffic Light'

It's along similar lines, but opens up more opportunity for a flowing discussion. This works with most students, but there are some out there who prefer a more direct approach and just want to be told what's going wrong and how they can I put it right!

If a student invites this as a coaching solution to the instructor, there's no harm in accepting the invitation, providing it's done with a degree of sensitivity.

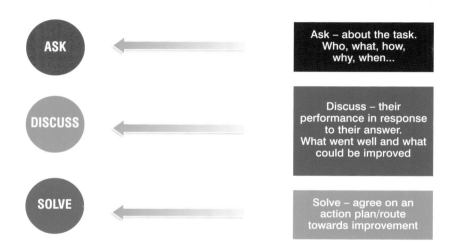

1. Ask the student about aspects of their performance. Start with open and general questions, then focus in on specific areas of performance.
2. Discuss these areas using the response to the questions given by the student.
3. Solve any problems firstly by encouraging the student to seek the solution. If they can't, the instructor will do this for them. However, the student should always be the one who identifies the problem and then provides the solution with guidance and help from the instructor.

By allowing the student to start analysing their performance of the skills being taught, then seeking ways of improving their performance, the students will learn how to continue this process after they have left the environment of the structured session led by an instructor.

In effect, the instructor is preparing the student for when the instructor is no longer there. After this training, the student should be able to continue with their own progress using the skills and learning process delivered by the instructor.

ASSESSING YOUR STUDENTS' ABILITIES

There is an element of assessment in every RYA training course, not just the formal assessment that leads to the award of a certificate but also the more informal assessment that takes place throughout the course, no matter how short or long it may be. Assessment is about understanding how the student is performing against a set of standards or expectations.

This might be summarised in three stages:

• Initial assessment.

• Formative assessment.

• Summative assessment.

For example, when an instructor or coach first meets their students an 'initial assessment' takes place where the instructor tries to establish what experience and skills the students already have. This initial assessment may be a simple discussion of previous sailing experience or it may be slightly more formal by asking students to set out on paper what they have done previously. The first on-water session is also used to establish the starting point for the course. The benefit of this approach is to enable the instructor to structure the course and the content to suit the students' actual levels of ability rather than their assumed level. There may also be formal checks to be made on pre-course requirements for instructor training.

As the course progresses the instructor will be carefully monitoring students' progress to see if the pace is too fast, too slow or just right to be challenging, informative and achievable. This can be described as the 'formative assessment' and once again could be either formal or informal. Group discussions, quizzes and one to one discussions may be useful here.

Finally, at the end of the course the instructor or coach has to decide, with the help of the Chief Instructor or senior instructor, whether or not the objectives of the training have been achieved. This is the 'summative assessment' and once again could use a range of methods to achieve an objective view of the assessment criteria. Practical tests, such as sailing around a triangular course without an instructor on board, are useful, as are quizzes, oral questions and more formal tests. Ultimately the question may be whether to award the certificate or not. To help you in this the following statements or measures may be of use but never forget that most people are doing this for fun and recognising the progress that your students have made by the award of certificates is more likely to motivate them to continue than withholding the certificate because they cannot perform the task every time!

CERTIFICATES

RYA certificates provide a great incentive to continue training, providing a clear measure of an individual's progress. However, they can become a discouragement to the weak student as the prospect of gaining a certificate fades. The Chief Instructor will advise on the importance of keeping everyone informed of their progress through the course, and what they can realistically achieve. This could involve breaking the news that a Performance Sailing certificate is not possible by the end of the course. The instructor should explain what can be achieved and agree with the student how to get the best possible value out of the course.

From then on, the instructor should set goals, point out strengths and weaknesses and offer encouragement. They should point out how much has been achieved as the course progresses so that by the final debrief both can be satisfied that the course was worthwhile.

If students are not kept informed, tension will build up with students discussing amongst themselves whether they are passing or failing. During the final debrief, instructor teaching may be blamed for lack of results. This lack of communication between instructor and student is one of the most common reasons for complaints about RYA courses. Remember that many of the people taught are highly successful and respected in their own field. The only skill the instructor may have that they haven't is the ability to sail and teach sailing. Ensure they retain their dignity and a positive attitude towards their instructor and the sport. This is one of the most skilful aspects of instructing.

The National Sailing Scheme & Youth Sailing Scheme

NATIONAL SAILING SCHEME OVERVIEW

The overall aim of the RYA National Sailing Scheme will always be to introduce and promote the sport of sailing in a safe, enjoyable and informative way. Consequently, it is considered more important that students enjoy their experience and improve their performance rather than the scheme striving for the highest possible standards of excellence. At the end of their course, students should understand the content, whilst possibly still making mistakes in their performance. This should not prevent them from being awarded a certificate. As a guide, if a student can, for example, in picking up a mooring use the correct speed, angle and sail setting in their approach but still miss picking up the buoy, they should have the section signed off in their logbook. If a student makes a lee shore landing at full speed under full sail crashing into the beach or pontoon, this indicates that they haven't fully understood what is required of the manoeuvre and will need further practice and input before they can be signed off.

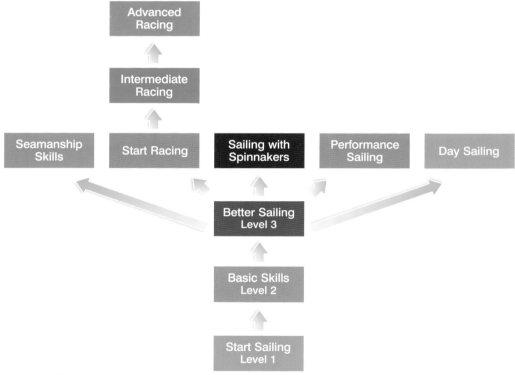

Level 1 Start Sailing

Aim To enjoy basic skills under relaxed tuition.

Content Basic practical elements.

Assessment Demonstrate the skill whilst being taught.

Level 2 Basic Skills

Aim To sail the dinghy after tuition without additional input from the instructor.

Content Rig and launch the dinghy. Sail a triangular course, pick up a mooring/MOB, come alongside and return safely to shore.

Assessment Continuous, showing an awareness of the 5 essentials. Safe, sound judgement is of a higher priority than perfect sail setting. Theory sections can be answered orally.

Level 3 Better Sailing

Aim To practise and be coached on the techniques and skills introduced in L1 Start Sailing and L2 Basic Skills and to be introduced to taster sessions of some new techniques from the advanced modules.

Content Improve skills and practise the five essentials. Taster sessions from the advanced modules such as Sailing with Spinnakers, Racing or Seamanship Skills.

Assessment By the end of the course the sailor should be able to sail confidently without an instructor on board in light to moderate breezes and have developed a better technical competence of basic skills.

Seamanship Skills

Aim To be able to carry out seamanship techniques in moderate wind conditions.

Content Often considered to be the 'stopping' skills e.g. coming alongside a jetty/vessel, MOB, anchoring, lee shore landing, heaving to, reefing afloat.

Assessment Continuous. Although students are not expected to demonstrate the skills first time, every time, a degree of understanding and consistency is expected. Some training centres have theory papers to help with assessments. If asked to assess one of these, study the paper in order to become familiar with the depth of knowledge required and ensure that all answers will be correct.

Day Sailing

Aim To be able to plan and embark upon a short day cruise.

Content Planning the cruise using relevant information and materials relating to charts, tides and weather.

Assessment Continuous, based on the success of the plan and trip. Any aspects not able to be covered can be judged by an oral session ashore.

Sailing with Spinnakers

Aim To be able to successfully use an asymmetrical/traditional spinnaker.

Content Preparation and rigging the spinnaker, hoist/drop techniques, gybing, trimming whilst underway.

Assessment Based mainly on understanding of the techniques. Instructors should provide intensive input and practice to improve students' performance.

Start Racing

Aim To provide knowledge, skills and confidence to the novice racer from a club environment.

Content The start line, starting and finishing, effective upwind sailing, mark rounding, effective downwind sailing, racing rules.

Assessment An understanding and awareness of his basic obligations to others and able to control his boat around the course in light to moderate conditions.

Performance Sailing

Aim How to sail performance boats to best advantage at all times.

Content Boat set up, use of all its controls and sails, coping with different wind conditions, remain upright, deal with capsizes and emergencies.

Assessment The emphasis is on coaching to improve the candidate's sailing performance. For instructors, this will involve coaching from powerboats. The course is intended primarily for two person spinnaker boats. However it may be delivered in performance single handers and the certificate endorsed accordingly.

Additional Racing Modules

Intermediate Racing

A programme to build on your basic racing skills and develop greater awareness of the key principles of starting boat handling, boat speed, strategy and tactics. This is predominantly a practical course.

Advanced Racing

Developing skills in preparation for open meetings and higher level competition. This is predominantly a practical course.

YOUTH SAILING SCHEME OVERVIEW

The syllabi for each of the four stages of the RYA Youth Sailing Scheme are clearly expressed in terms of competencies. As the student is able to do each item, so it can be signed off. There is provision for some guidance and help to be given within the Youth Sailing Scheme. When all the items for a particular award are complete, the certificate or sticker may be given. On any course, it is possible that some students will complete some extra items from the next stages, in which case those items can also be signed off.

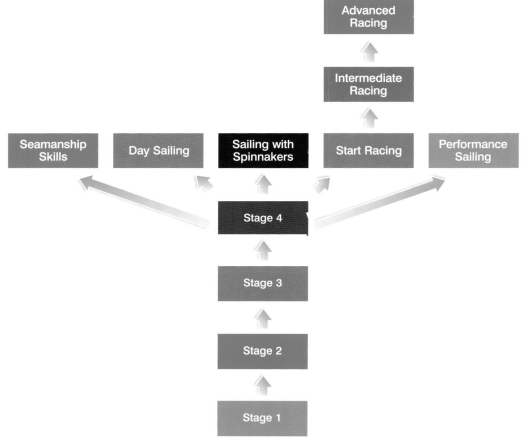

Stage 1

By the end of this introductory course, the student will have a basic understanding of how a boat sails, and some experience of steering and handling the boat. Stages 2, 3 and 4 will complete your introduction to the sport in easy stages.

Stage 2

By the end of this course, the student will have a range of sailing skills and background knowledge, and be well on the way to being a confident small boat sailor.

Stage 3

Having completed Stage 3 you will be able to sail in any direction and rig and launch your boat. Your skills and knowledge mean that you can regard yourself as a sailor, not a beginner.

Stage 4

A Stage 4 certificate means that you have the skills to sail a double-handed boat as crew or helm, and solve a variety of problems afloat. Passing this course is the natural entry point for the advanced courses.

Seamanship Skills – See page 49.

Day Sailing – See page 49.

Sailing with Spinnakers – See page 49.

Start Racing – See page 49.

Performance Sailing – See page 49.

Additional Racing Modules – See page 49.

GAMES TO FACILITATE LEARNING

Youth sailing courses invariably go well when some games are incorporated into the training programme. Games not only provide enjoyment and social interaction but also enable children to practise their sailing skills in a less formal environment. The following are examples of games designed to reinforce sailing skills.

Orienteering Afloat

As for land orienteering by using buoys marked with code letters.

Teaching points: Sailing on all points of the wind.

Resources: Buoys coloured or marked with code letters.

Tag

One boat is 'it', raises dagger board half way, throws tennis ball at other boats. If it hits, then struck boat is 'it', retrieves tennis ball, raises dagger board half-way and chases other boats. Useful to play when using different types of boats – Oppies and Toppers.

Teaching points: Use of centre/dagger board, speed control.

Resources: Tennis ball, large buoyant sponge, buoyant frisbee.

Relays

Team event to transport baton/piece of equipment/person from one shore to another. Variations: transport to a boat, race round a slalom course, collect gear required for a task. All of these need very clear instructions about changeover procedures, what and how objects can be carried, time penalties etc.

Teaching points: Sailing accurately on all points of sailing, landing on lee shore, leaving lee shore.

Resources: Buckets, tennis balls, corks.

All Standing Race

Race around a triangular course without sitting down in the boat (tack by walking around the mast or by stepping between boom and sail foot: gybe by stepping around sail clew).

Teaching points: Boat balance and trim.

Resources: Three buoys.

Treasure Hunt

Mix clues both onshore and on-the-water. Have each team follow a completely different order of clues. End with a picnic or barbecue when the 'treasure' is discovered. (Have some treasure for everyone, not just the first team.) Add to the fun with pirate costumes!

Teaching points: Accurate and fast sailing, team building.

Resources: Laminated clue sheets, face paints, box of dressing up clothes, 'treasure'.

The RYA Method covers the practical techniques of basic boat handling in the Start Sailing, Basic Skills and Better Sailing courses as well as Stages 1-4 in the Youth Sailing Scheme. Whilst the majority of the teaching method is appropriate for all three boat disciplines, some elements may not be e.g. capsize drill for keelboats.

The standardised teaching techniques enable Instructors to move from one centre to another and teach any part of the appropriate RYA course. Students can follow a course at one centre with a higher level course elsewhere, and the Instructors will know exactly what has been covered and what needs to be taught next.

The RYA Method analyses the various elements that make up the activity of sailing a small boat, splitting each element into simple stages. Emphasis is placed on revision and testing to ensure that each stage has been successfully learnt.

To maintain motivation, it is important that students succeed at each stage, so the pace of learning and the complexity of the task are adapted to the individual. Students are encouraged to work out solutions from basic 'models' supplied by the Instructor. In educational terms, it is a student-centred method based on experiential learning. When teaching beginners, different centres may use slightly different variations of the Method but all retain the basic philosophy. Thus the RYA Instructor should find no difficulty in adapting to local differences or 'house rules' within the basic framework.

The instructor course concentrates on the detail of the Method but the overall aim remains the same – to get students sailing safely on their own as soon as possible. Each technique is broken down into easy steps for learning but, once learnt, those steps should disappear as the manoeuvre becomes a continuous flowing action.

A student who, having mastered a technique effectively, then adapts what he has been taught to suit himself should never be criticised because he has departed from the Method. He should be encouraged to move on and learn more.

The following outline of the Teaching Method provides the sequence of sessions and the important teaching points. The training course will expand on this framework. When actually using the Method to teach beginners, some sessions may well be run together, but it is worth establishing the principle, that after only 20 minutes or so, the average student's ability to absorb information falls off considerably. A short break, followed by revision and informal testing, makes for much more efficient learning.

Training in the RYA Method avoids technical terminology. 'Ropes, seats, push and pull' are preferable to instructions which are complicated by unfamiliar terms. Students will be having enough trouble working out what is going on without being told to 'sheet out and bear away'. Some nautical terms in common use come naturally, however, so they will almost certainly be used and learnt in the first sessions.

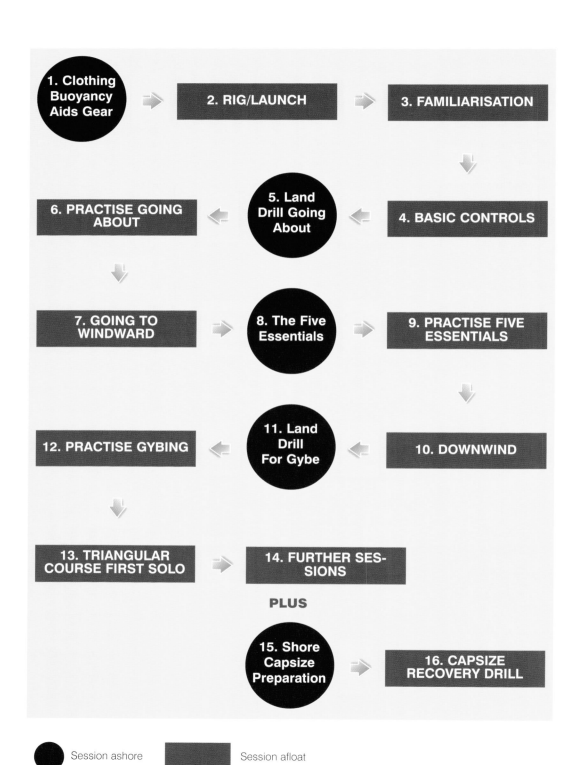

1. Clothing Buoyancy Aids Gear

2. RIG/LAUNCH

3. FAMILIARISATION

4. BASIC CONTROLS

5. Land Drill Going About

6. PRACTISE GOING ABOUT

7. GOING TO WINDWARD

8. The Five Essentials

9. PRACTISE FIVE ESSENTIALS

10. DOWNWIND

11. Land Drill For Gybe

12. PRACTISE GYBING

13. TRIANGULAR COURSE FIRST SOLO

14. FURTHER SESSIONS

PLUS

15. Shore Capsize Preparation

16. CAPSIZE RECOVERY DRILL

Session ashore   Session afloat

Session 1

Clothing/Footwear/Buoyancy aids/Gear collection

- Appropriate clothing: wetsuit, dry suit, waterproofs.
- Footwear: wet boots, trainers.
- Buoyancy aid: 50 Newtons, correct size, securely fastened, 150 Newtons life jackets for non-swimmers.
- Gear collection: identify each item briefly.

Session 2

Rigging/Launching

Rigging:

- Rig boat quickly, head to wind.
- Involve students.
- Explain briefly.
- Reef if necessary.

Launching and under way:

- Don't waste time.
- Hoist main.
- Keep students dry (where possible).

Top Tip

Most modern boats need jib up first for rig tension. Don't let it flog!

Furl/back it while preparing the rest of the dinghy.

Session 3

Familiarisation

Give your students time to absorb the sensation of being in a sailing boat perhaps for the first time. They should be looking out of the dinghy and not inside, enjoying the new sensation of being afloat. The session demonstrates your skill and, by making no demands of your students, allows everyone to start relaxing.

- Interesting, enthusiastic and enjoyable.
- Instructor at helm.
- Students allocated tasks.
- Students balance boat and gain awareness of wind direction and orientation.
- Short session.
- Calm, relaxed and controlled.
- Point out landmarks and wind direction.
- Sail a figure of 8 course.

Session 4

Basic Boat Controls

- Lying-to.
- Students take helm with target to aim at.
- Instructor sits to leeward and forward of the helmsman.
- Instructor keeps hands off the tiller while student is on the helm.
- Simple instructions such as 'pull it towards you/ push it away'.

> **Top Tip**
>
> Demonstrate good boat control whilst sailing,
> balance the boat and sails, then take your hand
> off the tiller to demonstrate that the boat
> continues sailing in a straight line.

Demonstrate basic boat controls:
- From lying-to position pull mainsail to turn boat towards wind.
- From lying-to, pull jib in to turn away from wind.

Relate changes in boat direction to the direction of the wind.
- Students practise.
- Discreetly moving your weight may be necessary to guarantee success.
- Effect of raising centre board.
- Point out 'no-go-zone' when tacking through 180 degrees.

Session 5

Tacking/Going About

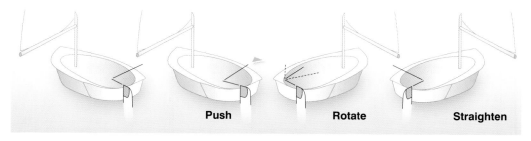

Push   **Rotate**   **Straighten**

The basics – Turning into the Wind and through 180 degrees
- Not all students will require a land drill, which is best done on a boat ashore.
- Demonstrate using the 'whole-part-whole' method.

The process is as follows:

1. Begin with the boat flat. If the sheeting arrangement is from the transom the helmsman changes hands on the extension and mainsheet.
2. The turn is initiated by easing the tiller extension smoothly away.
3. As boom nears the centreline, helmsman starts to move across boat, facing forwards if the boat is centre main rigged or aft if transom rigged.
4. Helmsman revolves extension away from him forward of the tiller. If the extension is too long to pass between the end of the tiller and the centre falls it will have to be swung towards the stern and over the tiller. This is done by sliding the hand down the extension, swivelling it around, and sliding the hand back up to the end.

5. As boom reaches new leeward quarter, helmsman centralises tiller as boat points towards new target and mainsail fills, and sits down. (If the boat is transom rigged, then the turn is complete.)

6. He then changes hands at this point by bringing the sheet hand back across in front of his body to hold both tiller extension and sheet. He takes the mainsheet with his front hand, releases sheet with back hand, bringing extension under arm to front of body.

Teaching the basics of tacking 180 degrees through the wind.

Very few students will absorb all the information listed above in one go. Teach the skills a little at a time, progressively adding bits in. A 'teaching summary' might therefore be:

Before turning

- Check the area to windward.
- Warn your crew calling 'Ready about'.

Then

1. Ease the tiller away from you, towards the sail.
2. As the boat turns under the boom, begin to move across to the other side.
3. Extend the tiller arm.
4. Sit down on the new side.
5. As the sail fills straighten the tiller.

Whether the boat is centre or aft mainsheet rigged the basic process is the same.

Notes

- At the start of the manoeuvre the boat should be flat.
- If you are tacking a centre mainsheet boat change hands when the tack is complete. Face forward during the manoeuvre.
- If you are tacking an aft mainsheet boat change hands before you push the tiller away. Face aft during the manoeuvre.
- In some boats the tiller extension may have to be rotated over the transom.

During the learning period the instructor will be responsible for the full control of the boat, instructing the crew and choosing the appropriate time and place to turn. Once the process is mastered the instructor can pass control over to the student.

The student helmsman will then have to:

- Decide when it is appropriate to tack.
- Check area into which he is going to sail.
- Warn the crew by calling 'Ready about'.
- As he eases the tiller extension firmly away call 'Lee oh'.

Train the crew to take the following action as the boat is turned:

- When the helmsman calls 'Ready about' the crew uncleats jib sheet and checks area.
- When he is ready, he answers 'Ready' to the call 'Ready about'.
- As the boom reaches the centreline crew takes up slack in new jib sheet and moves across boat.
- As the mainsail fills crew sheets in jib.

Top Tip

Choose obvious targets for students to sail towards after tacking.

Going About – the Complete Manoevuvre

Going About Aft Mainsheet

The helmsman faces aft during the manoeuvre and uses the frying pan grip (palm up thumb on top), and before tacking he looks into the area where he is going to tack into to make sure that it is clear, and keeps the boat flat.

1. Helmsman "flicks" the spare mainsheet to the back of the boat under the tiller. Front hand holding the mainsheet, the back hand on the tiller and says "Ready about".

2. Crew checks, and if clear says "Ready".

Helmsman changes hands on mainsheet and tiller extension by trapping the mainsheet under the thumb of the rear hand and picking up the tiller extension with the front hand.

3. Helm initiates the turn by easing the tiller away smoothly, saying "Lee oh".

4. As the boom reaches the leeward stern quarter, the crew releases the jib sheet.

5. As the boom nears the centre line, the helm starts to move across the boat, front foot leading. About this time the crew can also start to move.

6. Helmsman rotates tiller extension away from him forward of the tiller, and steps fully onto the new windward side. Crew picks up new jib sheet and balances boat.

7. As the boom reaches the new leeward quarter, both helm and crew move to sit down. Helm centralises the tiller as the mainsail starts to fill. Crew sheets in the jib.

8. Boat sails on, crew balancing the boat, the helm making small tiller/mainsheet adjustments where necessary.

Going About Centre Mainsheet

The helmsman faces forwards through the manoeuvre, not moving too quickly across the boat, helping the balancing action. The helm holds the tiller and mainsheet in the "dagger/dagger" grip.

1. Helmsman sails the boat flat, and checks into the area where the boat will be turning into. If it is clear, helm calls "Ready about". Helm checks that spare mainsheet is untangled. Crew uncleats jib and when ready says "Ready".

2. Helm calls "Lee oh" and eases the mainsail a little while pushing away gently. The rear leg is extended across towards the middle of the boat.

3. As the boat sails up into the wind the crew releases the jib.

4. Helm rotates the end of the tiller extension forwards, out to the side of the boat and then as the boom moves across to the leeward side, straightens the tiller onto the centreline of the boat steering with the hand holding the tiller behind his back. The helm balances the boat before moving further. The crew sheets in the jib on the new side.

5. Helm rotates the end of the tiller in the palm of the hand so that the thumb is uppermost and sits down, steering behind his back.

6. The helm brings the hand holding the mainsheet up to the tiller extension, thumb extended and trapping the sheet against the extension. The thumbs of both hands point towards each other.

7. Helm releases the tiller with the front hand, and moves the arm back across the front of the body to take hold of the mainsheet, and when in a firm grasp it can be released by the back hand.

8. With the boat balanced and under control, the back hand holding the tiller can be brought up under the armpit to finish in front of the body.

9. The boat sails on under control. Continue to practise until instruction is no longer needed.

Tacking Method – Variations

There are several variations for centre mainsheet boats in addition to the basic one outlined previously.

Many modern boats have such long tiller extensions that the tiller extension will not fit past the mainsheet hoop/falls (e.g. RS400, Laser Stratos). In this case simply slide your tiller hand down the extension as you move into the boat (preventing over-steering) and rotate the extension around the back of the boat over the transom. After crossing the boat, proceed using one of the following methods.

With the boat flat, the helm alters the position of the tiller extension so that the end of the extension is pointing up over the rearmost shoulder. All other commands are as for the basic method tack.

As the tiller is pushed away, the helm also starts to rotate the end of the tiller extension out over the transom past the end of the boom until the tiller extension is pointing out over the opposite side of the boat and the helm now stands to cross the boat.

Helm and crew complete the tack as for the normal centre mainsheet tacking method.

Date	Course	Price	Time	Description	Age
22-23 Mar / 4-5 Oct	Powerboat Level 2	£250.00	10:00-16:30	to teach boat handling and seamanship in powerboats. Pre-requisite for Dinghy instructor and Windsurf Start instructor courses.	16+
29 Mar / 27 Sept	One Day Emergency 1st Aid	£80.00	9:00-17:00	Level 2 Emergency First Aid at Work (EFAW) Pre-requisite for any instructor course.	16+
11 Oct or 12 Oct	RYA Dinghy Instructor Pre-entry Assessment	£40.00	10:00-16.30	Pre-requisite for Dinghy Instructor Course – You will require a G14 for this assessment and it sets out what you will be assessed on.	16+
14-18 May	RYA Start Windsurf Instructor	£250.00	9:00-18:00	Qualify to teach junior syllabus and beginner adult courses. Prerequisites – Intermediate, Non Planning, Beach Start, 1st Aid and powerboat Level 2.	16+
25 Apr	BSUPA Stand-Up Paddling Instructor	£80.00	9:00-17:00	Qualify as a BSUPA Stand-Up Paddleboarding Instructor. One day instructor certification for individuals with an existing instructor qualification.	16+
29 Oct-2 Nov	Dinghy Instructor	£250.00	9:00-17:00	You will receive training in teaching techniques afloat and ashore during the instructor training course. Pre-requisite - Pre-entry Assessment, 1st Aid and Powerboat Level 2.	16+

To book call 01285 860388

South Cerney Outdoor

Lake 12, Spine Road, South Cerney, Gloucestershire, GL7 5TL
Email: southcerneyoutdoor@prospects.co.uk

www.southcerneyoutdoor.co.uk

Instructor Courses 2014...

We have created the best instructor courses we can in order to maintain the highest standard. We have a full range of equipment to use with excellent teaching facilities and very experienced qualified coaches.

Date	Activity	Cost	Time	Activity/Requirements	Age
18–21 Mar	UKCC Level 1 Paddle Sport Coach	£230.00	9:30-17:00	The Level 1 is the first step on the Paddlesport Coaching Pathway. The qualification introduces new coaches to the concepts of good coaching practice and understanding of the technical elements of the sport. • Adult 2* • FSRT • Registered with BCU	16+
21–24 Oct	UKCC Level 2 Paddle Sport Coach Training	£230.00	9:30-17:00	The award develops the foundation coaching skills taught at Level 1 that will underpin their future coaching behaviours and practice. Aiming to develop skills that will benefit any paddler irrespective of what boat they are paddling. • Level 1 Paddlesport Coach • 3* in one discipline • Registered with BCU	16+
2-6 Jun	UKCC Level 1 Paddle Sport Coach	£230.00	10:30-17:00	The Level 1 is the first step on the Paddlesport Coaching Pathway. • Adult 2* • FSRT	16+

Session 6

Practise Going About (through 180 degrees)

After practice the student should be able to sail around a shallow figure of eight course, going about at each end, without any help from the Instructor.

• Go about from reach to reach. Practise often.
• Ensure boat is going fast enough to tack through 180 degrees.
• Check crew and jib position.
• Consider a land drill if necessary.

Session 7

Going to Windward

Going to windward and developing tacking through an increasingly narrow angle until tacking close hauled to close hauled through 90 degrees is achieved.

In fluctuating winds, sailing on a close reach initially will make life easier for your students.

• Demonstrate that the sails flap as boat turns towards the wind.
• Demonstrate the no-go-zone again.
• Demonstrate and explain the concept of beating to windward.
• Take the boat downwind. Hand over to the student and ask to be sailed to a point directly upwind.

Many students will now be able to do this unaided so only intervene if you feel that it is really necessary.

• Don't worry if the tacking is inefficient.
• Use the flapping of the jib luff as an indicator of the edge of the no-go-zone.
• Relate progress to landmarks.
• Check ability to determine wind direction.
• Stress that the angle between the sails and the wind stays the same wherever the boat is pointing.

Tacking will now be through 90 degrees although the novice may tack from close reach to close reach initially. Tacking can be developed further by rolling the boat through the tack.

• Ensure the boat is flat.
• Crew bring their weight inboard to initiate turn.
• The boat will turn towards the wind as it heels.
• Steer through the wind but discourage over-steering.
• Crew's feet are brought under the body as the boat turns.
• The mainsail is eased.
• Helm and crew move across together and sit out.
• The boat is brought upright and the mainsail sheeted in.

> **Top Tip**
>
> When sailing to windward, sit well forward.

Sessions 8 & 9

The Five Essentials

The five essentials contain the core skills required to sail a boat properly.

1 Sail Setting

• Restate the point regarding the angle between the sails and the wind.
• Simple board sketch or a working model.
• Sails should be 'just not flapping'. Ease sails when turning away from the wind and sheet in when turning.
• Remind students to sheet out when bearing away.
• Consider using tell tales.

> **Top Tip**
>
> The Five Essentials should form a continuous thread at every level. Comment on all five whatever the theme of the session.

2 Balance

- Sail upright for minimum drag.
- Demonstrate afloat how heeling makes the boat turn.
- Every rudder movement slows the boat.
- Remember 'balance affects turning'.

3 Boat Trim

- Show trim for different points of sailing. Explain why the boat goes better close-hauled with weight forward and better off the wind with weight back.
- Remember 'trim affects speed'.

4 Centreboard

- Demonstrate settings for different points of sailing and different classes of boats.

5 Course made good

- Explain different courses that will take you to windward. If the students are ready, introduce the idea that one course may be better than another because of tide, wind shadows or hazards – all in a very basic form.
- Encourage students to make their own decisions based on personal observation.

Session 10

Downwind

- Teach the students how to bear away using a combination of slight windward heel, letting out the mainsheet and avoid over-steering.
- Demonstrate the difference between a training run and a dead run using the jib to indicate the difference between the two.
- Allow plenty of room (wind against tide is ideal).
- Students practise running, turning from a beam reach, through a broad reach to a training run and then back to close-hauled.
- Any change in direction requires changes in the Five Essentials.
- Avoid gybing at this stage.
- End this session with a smooth controlled demonstration gybe.

Session 11

Gybing

Similar to tacking, learning the technique can be divided into various component parts:

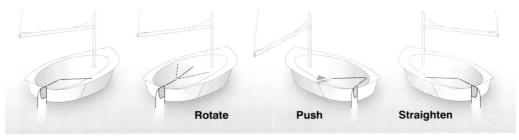

Rotate   **Push**   **Straighten**

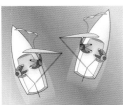

- Explain fundamental difference between tacking and gybing.
- Stress the very clear difference in commands – 'Ready about' for tacking but 'Stand by to gybe' for gybing which avoids any possible confusion.
- Using smooth and deliberate actions will help success.

Gybing – Aft Mainsheet

Not all students will require a land drill, which is best done on a boat or land trainer ashore.

Any demonstration should use the "whole-part-whole" method.

1.

2.

3.

4.

5.

6.

1. With the boat being sailed flat on a training run, the helm sits forward of the tiller extension. All checks are made to ensure that:
- Centreboard is only slightly down
- The jib is just starting to collapse
- The area in which the boat is about to turn into is clear
- Helm says "Stand by to gybe"
- Crew checks and says "Yes"
- Helm sheets in the mainsail slightly to bring the boom clear of the shroud.

2. Helm swaps hand on the tiller and mainsheet.

3. Balancing the boat, helm moves to the middle of the boat without altering the steering, one foot either side of the centreboard casing front foot leading.

4. Before initiating the gybe, the helm swings the end of the tiller extension forwards out over the opposite side to the boom.
Helm calls "Gybe oh" and initiates gybe by pushing the tiller towards where he was sitting and waits for the boom to swing across.

5. As the mainsail clew lifts and starts to travel across the boat, the helm centralises the tiller so that his weight, the boom and tiller are simultaneously in the middle of the boat. The crew changes over the jib sheet, and moves to the centre of the boat. Note that the boat is still flat.

6. The helm sits down on the new windward side. The crew sets the jib on the new side.

Gybing – Centre Mainsheet

The important difference about this drill is that the helmsman takes hold of the falls of the mainsheet to guide the boom across, preventing a violent gybe.

1.

2.

3.

4.

5.

6.

1. While on a training run, the helmsman balances the boat as necessary, and checks all around, especially into the area in which the boat is turning through and into. Helm holds the tiller extension in the dagger grip and calls "Stand by to gybe". Crew checks the area and says "Yes".

2. Helm steps back foot forward into the middle of the boat whilst at the same time revolving the tiller extension over to the new side whilst still steering a straight course.

3. Helm holds the falls of the mainsheet, the crew moves into the centreline of the boat and changes the jib sheets.

4. Helm calls "Gybe oh" and initiates the gybe by pushing the tiller extension towards where he was sitting and waits for the boom to start to move. Helm can assist by guiding boom with the falls.
As soon as the boom starts to move, the helm centralises the tiller and prepares to sit down on the new windward side. Crew balances the boat.

5. As the boom nears the centreline of the boat the helm, with weight evenly on both feet and the tiller, is in the middle of the boat.

6. As the boom continues on its way over the boat, the helm releases the falls.

7.

8.

9.

10.

11.

7. Still steering a straight course, the helm transfers his weight over to the new windward side.
   Crew changes the jib fully onto the new side and prepares to move across to the windward side to assist with boat balance.

8. Helm sits and steers the boat on its new course (training run) with the tiller hand behind his back.

9. Helmsman brings sheet hand back across in front of body to hold both tiller extension and sheet, thumb pointing towards end of tiller extension.

10. Releasing the tiller with his front hand, he reaches forward and takes the mainsheet, releasing the sheet from his back hand. He can then bring extension under the back arm to in front of body. Facing and momentarily leaning forward will help this action.

11. Helm trims the mainsheet and settles on new course.

Gybe – Method Variations

- The variations in handling the tiller extension are the same as for tacking.
- With long tiller extensions, slide your hand down the extension before the gybe to reduce the angle through which you push the tiller.
- Holding the 'falls' of the mainsheet to help the sail across only works with a 'true' centre main. Aft/Centre combinations can benefit from a pull on the sheet (e.g. Laser) but will not have the same effect.

Session 12

Gybing Practice

- Consider reefing.
- Allow plenty of room (wind against tide if possible).
- Check the area to be sailed into.
- Use minimal steering.
- The helmsman should make a positive movement to initiate the gybe.
- Stress that the mainsail should be brought off the shroud.

Session 13

Triangular Course First Solo

- Triangular course: with achievable windward leg.
- Initially sail with students and then move into the safety boat, but allow them time to 'settle'.
- Give instruction where necessary but avoid shouting from the safety boat. Ask them to 'lie-to' to communicate.
- Remember you are still responsible for the safety of the boat and crew.

Session 14

Further Sessions

The purpose of the 'development exercises' section is to continue to develop the students' boat handling skills through practice, in particular positioning and stopping, which will be useful when the students are returning to base. The instructor should always be afloat in a safety boat and on hand to offer coaching input whenever necessary.

The instructor has introduced various techniques and now the student needs the opportunity to practise these techniques in order to be more skilful.

The instructor should have a variety of exercises available that help the student practise the techniques they have learned. The use of exercises such as those contained in G100 RYA Race Training Exercises is really helpful. When setting courses for students, remember that you need to be able to communicate with them throughout using some of the techniques explained in the single handers' section.

Awareness of other boats will have been part of your teaching in the early stages. Stress it again now. Discuss 'rule of the road' problems as they occur and your solo crew will be less likely to become involved in collisions.

Top Tip

Once you step out of the boat, things can go wrong for the student. Give them time to settle.

Sessions 15 & 16

Capsize Recovery Drill (scoop method for dinghy)

Capsize recovery drill should fit into your programme at the earliest practical moment. Weather, water temperature and other considerations will influence your Senior Instructor's decision, but it is generally agreed that early capsizing is beneficial.

The end of a day's sailing provides the best opportunities for drying clothes, personal buoyancy and gear. Students are usually apprehensive about capsizing, and that apprehension can affect their ability to learn. Once capsizing is over, they learn more quickly and are less worried. They are more likely to succeed when they go 'solo'.

During the capsize drill, the responsibility of the instructor is to enter the water with the students because they have been with students constantly up to this point.

The students would consider it strange if their instructor abandoned them at this stage. Instructors cannot fully control the exercise from a safety boat, although it should, of course, be standing by. The drill must go smoothly and calmly to have the desired effect of building confidence.

• Always ensure that sufficient rescue cover is provided.
• Shore briefing or drill using a boat tipped on its side.
• Explain the scoop method.
• Check personal and boat buoyancy.
• Check students (contact lenses, glasses, watches and even false teeth!).
• Consider mast head flotation for training purposes.
• Your Senior Instructor is responsible for selecting a suitable site for the drill, away from hazards but close enough to base for safety and recovery.
• The instructor is responsible for tipping the boat over (wild swinging on the shrouds is unnecessary: a brisk tack with the mainsail sheeted well in and the crew staying on the old windward side of the boat should cause a gentle capsize).
• Smile, stay calm.
• Encourage students but keep any physical assistance to a minimum.
• The students will be much more confident if they have righted the boat without outside help.

Repeat the capsize until each student has succeeded but watch out for exhaustion or hypothermia problems after two or three attempts. It is better to stow the boat and gear after everyone has changed rather than risk difficulties with the cold. Maintain constant encouragement.

Top Tip

Allow for free floating in deep water (buoy the mast head). Tethers and mooring ropes can separate students from the boat.

Step 1

• Both the crew swim to the stern. This reduces the risk of one becoming trapped if the boat inverts.
• Helmsman checks that the rudder is secure and not floating off.
• Crew finds the end of the mainsheet and gives it to the helmsman who, using it as a lifeline, swims around the outside of the boat to the centreboard and holds it or climbs onto it as necessary to prevent inversion.
• Crew then swims along the inside of the boat to the centreboard case.

Following initial immersion, most students are still regaining their breath by the time the crew or helmsman has to go UNDER the mainsheet assembly to get clear round to the centreboard. Many try to swim over the top and some get their personal buoyancy hooked into the various floating bits of rope. Warn them of these difficulties.

Step 2

- The crew checks that the centreboard is fully down.
- Helmsman holds onto it to prevent the boat inverting.

If the centreboard is not fully down, warn the crew of the risk of injury to the helmsman from an over-enthusiastic attempt to lower it without warning.

Step 3

- Crew finds the top (weather) jib sheet and throws it over to the helmsman, checks mainsheet is free.
- Helmsman confirms that he has it.

Confirmation of receipt is often inaudible, especially if the helmsman has failed to receive it. The centreboard case is a useful slot through which to shout.

Step 4

Crew lies in the hull facing forwards and floats above the side-deck, holding on but taking care not to prevent the boat from righting.

Many students do not, initially, realise the great importance of this point. Some even disregard it, believing that they will be safer by hanging on.

Step 5

- Helmsman either lies back straight in the water with his feet on the boat's gunwale and hauls on the jib sheet.
- Alternatively he climbs onto the centreboard, keeping his weight as close to the hull as possible to avoid breaking the board, and hauls on the jib sheet to right the dinghy with the crew member in it.

Some find it difficult to get onto the centreboard. Any preliminary advice, which you can provide, is worth giving. Heavyweights will be able to right the dinghy by the first method. With lightweights, the advice to keep as close to the hull as possible has to be modified in practice, as their weight is sometimes insufficient to provide the necessary righting moment. Stress the value of straight legs and back for maximum leverage.

Top Tip

Face away from the boat and throw the jib sheet over your head – it's easier.

Step 6

- With the jib backed the boat is hove-to and the crew is then able to help the helmsman aboard.
- Helmsman may find that he can get into the boat as it comes upright.

The right place for the helmsman to be brought aboard is beside the weather shroud. Discuss the option of rolling the boat to windward if you have a lightweight crew and a heavyweight helmsman.

In boats with open transoms, it may be more practical to re-enter over the stern. The problem with this method is that the boat tends to bear away around the person hanging on to the stern, so a speedy entry is necessary.

Many modern boats have the buoyancy built into the floor and sides of the hull. This means that they can invert more readily after capsizing.

Alternative Method of Capsize Recovery

- At the point of capsize, the crew nearest the highest point of the hull steps over the gunwale and onto the centreboard as the rig hits the water.
- Their priority is to keep the mast level on the surface of the water, preventing the boat from inverting.
- At the same time, they check that the other crew member is present and is able to release the mainsheet and kicker to de-power the rig.
- If they can't detect the other crew's presence, their priority is to start bringing the boat upright, using their weight and leaning back against a jib or spinnaker sheet.
- If the crew is present, they can also check that the rudder is still attached to the boat, and that they are ready for the righting process to begin.
- The boat is then righted by the crew member on the centreboard leaning back and holding onto the sheets to help with this.
- As the boat passes through the point of pivot, the crew on the centreboard can step over the gunwale and back into the boat as the other crew is scooped up by the lower gunwale.
- If the rig is pointing into the wind, then the boat needs to be righted slowly to stop it passing through the upright position and capsizing again. This can be achieved by good communication and the crew on the centreboard warning whoever is in the water to lie along the length of the gunwale so that when the boat is brought up, that crew's weight will act as a 'damper', stopping the boat from rolling right over again.

ADDITIONAL PRACTICAL SESSIONS

In the course of the previous sessions students will have left and returned to base on several occasions. They can now go on to learn capsize drill, man overboard, picking up moorings, coming alongside a moored boat etc with more guidance and coaching. The instructor will be in and out of the boat, demonstrating particular skills and then watching progress from the shore or a safety boat.

A progression of these sessions could be:
- Leaving and returning to shore.
- MOB recovery.
- Picking up a mooring (small, soft, fixed target, with escape route).
- Coming alongside a moored safety boat (large, potentially hard target, with escape route).
- Coming alongside and leaving jetty/pontoon (large, hard target, limited escape route options).
- Lee shore landing (large, hard target with no escape route).

The generic skills for upwind approaches will be:
- Approaching from the downwind position (tide allowing).
- Slow the boat in good time by easing the sails early (no brakes).
- Maintain steerage and passage through the water by using small amounts of power from the sails when necessary.
- On arrival let the sail or sails out completely.

The generic skills for downwind approaches will be (or any of the above with a wind against tide situation):
- Approach from well upwind, throw the main halyard overboard and ensure that it streams freely.
- Turn head to wind, ease the kicker, take off the Cunningham, release the main halyard and drop the mainsail fully into the dinghy, removing the halyard from the headboard of the sail.
- Bear away and head for the beach (or chosen 'target') using the jib for power.
- Prior to arrival, raise the centreboard and release the rudder downhaul.
- In the shallows, release the jib, round up into wind allowing the crew to step out and secure the boat head to wind.

One of the more challenging skills of coming alongside a pontoon or jetty should be one of the last ones taught, and possibly avoided altogether if boats, crew and equipment could become damaged. This skill is perhaps better suited to being taught in the Seamanship Skills section.

Man Overboard Recovery (dinghy):

Use dummy (fender and tyre), not a real person.

• Regain control immediately and turn onto a beam reach.

• Maintain visual contact.

• Sail away on beam reach for 10/15 boat lengths, but do not lose sight of the MOB.

• Tack and bear away sharply.

• Position the dinghy so that final approach is on a close reach.

• Spill and fill the mainsail to control boat speed which should be slow on the final approach.

• Stop to leeward and immediately beside the MOB.

• Helmsman goes forward and retrieves the MOB by the windward shroud.

• A flick to windward on the tiller helps prevent the boat tacking on top of the MOB, who will act as a drogue or sea anchor to keep the dinghy in the basic hove-to position.

• Repeat with helmsman as MOB, i.e. crew takes control of the boat.

If it happened for real, the MOB should shout or whistle to gain attention but not swim about or he will rapidly lose body heat. If wearing personal buoyancy with additional oral inflation, he should inflate it, although it may need to be deflated for boarding.

Outline the aftercare needed for a real casualty.

Once your students have mastered the basic principles, encourage more realistic practice by briefing them that it should be the helmsman who 'falls overboard'. When the dummy is dropped over the side, the helmsman should let go of the tiller and mainsheet, move out of the way of the crew and take no further part in the manoeuvre. This results in the crew having to regain full control of the dinghy and achieves better results.

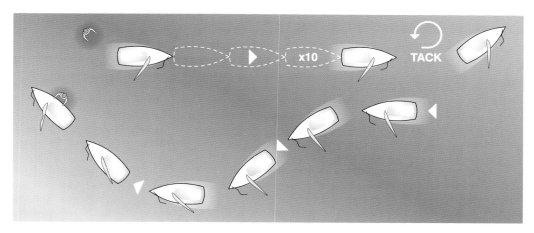

Fun Race

Some Senior Instructors like to finish a Level 2 course by a practical assessment in which the students sail around a triangular course. Many centres complete the Level 2 course by organising a small informal race, thus encouraging students to consolidate their skills and introducing them to the competitive side of the sport.

Assuming that you have covered the basic rules of the road, the minimum extra knowledge needed by students to complete this satisfactorily is an explanation of the typical port-hand triangular course and a basic starting procedure.

Top Tip

Never force people to be competitive when introducing racing to another course. Allow them to find their own level of competitiveness.

9 The RYA Teaching Method – Adaptations for Single Handers

Single handers are used in many centres and instructors should be familiar with the differences in teaching them.

General Points

Advantages of using single handers:

- Students continuously at the helm.
- They learn faster.
- Light.
- Simple and exciting.
- Particularly effective for teaching children.
- Less expensive to run.
- Durable.
- Low skill level required to succeed in some boats (Laser Funboat, Escape Mango).
- More economical teaching ratio (6:1).

Disadvantages of using single handers:

- Can be frustrating at first.
- Students tire easily.
- Communication is harder.
- Group control can be more difficult.
- Students become cold more quickly.
- Students may quickly scatter over a large area.

Sessions should be short and the instructor must always watch for signs of fatigue. Capsizes are more likely in a single hander than in the instructed larger dinghy, so suitable preparation must be made, as outlined below.

Teaching Equipment/Sailing Area

Instructors may have to adapt the equipment and select an appropriate sailing area to achieve the tasks set.

- Equipment – the right size of boat and sail area for the size of student.
- Wind strength.
- Wind direction.
- Air and water temperature.
- Sailing area.
- Depth of water (can the foils be full lowered?).
- Starting point (beach/pontoon/bank/slipway).
- Length of sessions (short).
- Any/other hazards.
- Tide.
- Instructor to check all boats before they go afloat.

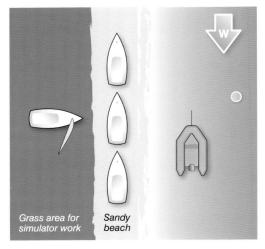

Grass area for simulator work   Sandy beach

Group Control

• Frequent regrouping and briefings.

• Recall signals (whistle and hand signals).

• Awareness of sailing area – diagrams, set course before students go afloat so they can see the boundaries.

• Question students to check understanding.

• Consider using a 'buddy system' when launching/recovering.

What If ... ?

Always consider:

• What is the worst thing that could happen?

• What changes can you make to cope with this?

• If you are starting to doubt that you can cope, stop and re-assess the session.

Communication

• Well thought out and structured briefings (include problems that might occur).

• Size of sailing area.

• You should not have to shout to your students.

• Students stop the boat and you go to them, or students come to you.

• Be aware of the noise from an engine or a sail flapping.

• Keep session short.

• Good debrief, which should include feedback to each student.

• Instructors may sail with the students providing they have the required safety cover available.

Capsize

Because your students are on their own and not very confident, you must point out:

• Righting a boat is easy.

• It can be fun.

• Wearing the right equipment means they will float in the water.

• Demonstration from instructor first to show how easy it is.

• Even on a hot sunny day your students can get cold once wet.

• Try to avoid capsize practice until the end of the day.

• Try to keep them as dry as possible (consider reefing).

• Land drill if possible.

Philosophy

The basic philosophy of the RYA Teaching Method outlined earlier applies just as much to single-handed teaching as to conventional techniques, but at any stage you should ask yourself two questions:

• What do students already know?

• What is the minimum they need to know before they can complete the next session successfully?

This should save you unnecessary time ashore and save you teaching irrelevant details.

SESSION OUTLINES

The programme given below is just one of many which have been developed successfully. It is not intended to be definitive, merely to provide an introduction to the techniques needed.

Think of the timing of your shore sessions. You have to cover a lot of teaching material. Usually your students should know how to turn, stop and deal with a capsize before going afloat.

Session 1

Clothing/Footwear/Buoyancy aids/
Gear collection:

* As for basic Method.
* Consider wet/dry suits and helmets.
* Correctly fitting buoyancy aids.

Session 2

Tacking land drill/getting out of irons (with a simulator):

* Establish wind direction.
* Demonstrate sailing on a beam reach, sheeting in and boat balance.
* Swing boat through the wind.
* Demonstrate tacking using the method (centre main or aft mainsheet).
* Each student should then practise.
* The instructor should then correct any faults.

Demonstrate getting out of irons (push/push, pull/pull)

Session 3

Rigging:

* Establish wind direction.
* Rig one boat first as a demonstration.
* Students can then rig their own boats.
* Check each one before they go afloat.

Session 4

Practise tacking/Beam reach/
Starting and stopping:

* Boats rigged.
* Demonstrate launching one boat.
* Instructor demonstrates what is to be done, sail out on beam reach, tack and return slowing down and raising the dagger board/rudder close to the beach.
* Remember, actions are more effective than words.
* Instructor in the water.
* Instructor demonstrates capsize drill.
* Check student's orientation is correct.
* Before letting go, go through sailing position, starting and stopping, tacking (walk boat through tack).
* Once ready send one dinghy off on way to buoy.
* Talk student through tack (student doesn't have to tack around the mark, near it will do).
* Talk student back to you, stopping the boat by you.
* Once each student has had a go, set up a beam reach figure of eight course.
* Add boats to the course one at a time, once it is clear that the preceding student is sailing/tacking successfully.
* Once the students have mastered the course, lengthen it.

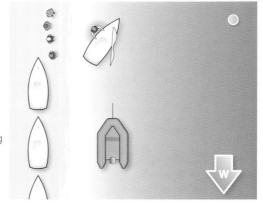

Session 5

Turning towards and away from the wind:

- Lay course as shown.
- Move buoy further into wind as session continues.
- Brief clearly using board or diagram.
- Demonstrate ashore or afloat the sail positions as boat turns towards and away from the wind.
- Reinforce wind direction at each step.
- Use easy steps for getting from beam reach to close-hauled.
- For bearing away, sheet out, use careful steering and boat balance.
- Students practise.
- Move buoy up in stages.
- Debrief ashore at end of session.

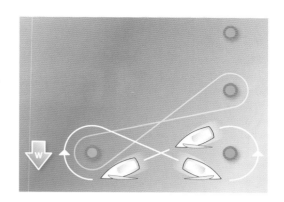

Session 6

Going to windward/bearing away and sailing downwind:

- Lay course similar to illustration, ensuring downwind course is a broad reach.
- Brief clearly using board or diagram.
- Reinforce no-go zone.
- Demonstrate in water or on simulator.
- Effects on sail.
- Revise luffing up and bearing away.
- Demonstrate.
- Send off students one at a time at intervals.
- Introduce the Five Essentials to this exercise.

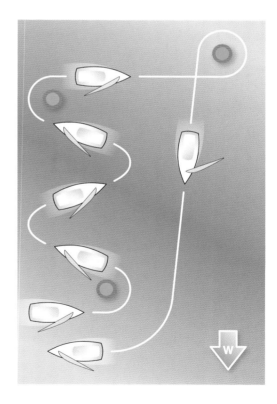

Session 7

Gybing Practice:

- Demonstrate on land using the method (centre main/aft main).
- Training run.
- Dagger board position.
- Reinforce Five Essentials.
- Allow each student to practise.

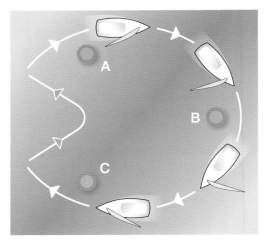

Session 8

Triangular Course:

- Lay course as shown.
- Demonstrate to students.
- Send students off one at a time at intervals.
- Move mark B towards the line between A and C until AB and BC become training runs.
- Avoid dead runs and 'death rolls' caused by 'sailing by the lee'.
- Debrief ashore.

Session 9

Follow my leader (behind safety boat, or another boat if helmed by a competent sailor).

- Lead boat sails a variety of courses.
- Following boats should tack/gybe where it turns, not when.
- Carry two drop marks in the safety boat.
- If there are any problems, drop the marks on a beam reach and instruct the fleet to sail a 'sausage course' around them while the problem is dealt with.

General Comments

- Keep sessions short and intensive.
- Clear briefings are essential.
- Debrief each session with effective feedback to individual students.
- Lay marks between sessions so your students can see the course before setting off.

> In ideal conditions, with above average students and good support, sessions 1 to 8 can be completed in a single long day. It is far more practical, however, to treat this as two days of instruction, which is the usual time taken for an RYA Level 1 course.

Further Sessions

Coming alongside:

- Same principles apply.
- Can only be achieved in wind against tide conditions by releasing the mainsail completely or releasing the clew.

Lee shore landings:

- Use similar principles as for double handers, but without the jib.
- It is important that the main is fully released either by unthreading the mainsheet or releasing the clew. Releasing the mainsheet only, reduces wear on the sail.
- Explain when to raise dagger board and rudder.

Manoeuvres such as collecting objects in the water, using the MOB technique and sailing up to moorings are good boat handling practice.

If your students are working towards their Level 2 certificate, you now have several days to consolidate the basic techniques and cover the onshore teaching and exercises etc afloat.

Teaching in Keelboats

The 'method' progression of learning to sail can be successfully taught in keelboats with a few simple modifications. Land drills are inappropriate, but the use of the boat controls for tacking and gybing can be demonstrated on a mooring.

The main differences from teaching in a dinghy are:

• The instructor will probably be teaching on board rather than from a safety boat.

• Allow students to take control if they are competent and avoid standing over them at the backstay.

• There are usually only four essentials.

• Techniques for grounding recovery.

• Use of engine.

• Man overboard technique.

• Use of harnesses.

With up to five students on board there is less helming time per person, although the crewing tasks are more involved. Move everyone around regularly. Little and often is appropriate for boat handling. For example, the group can practise picking up moorings by approaching on the correct point of sail without actually securing to the buoy. This allows you to teach the principles and gives everyone a try quickly, allowing for slight mis judgements.

Man Overboard

Small keelboats can use the dinghy method but for larger boats (where a man held in the water will not affect the drift of the boat) use one or both of the following:

Quick stop with engine:

• Shout 'Man overboard'.

• Pointer allocated, immediate heave to.

• Drop lifebelt and Dan buoy.

• Start engine, check no ropes overboard.

• Drop jib in hove-to position.

• Motor sail downwind until wind indicator points at man.

• Motor upwind.

• Retrieve man at shrouds keeping propeller clear.

Reach-tack-reach Man Overboard

• Pointer allocated.

• Immediate heave to.

• Drop lifebelt and Dan buoy.

• Sail away 10-15 boat lengths on apparent beam reach.

• Tack – can drop jib, furl jib or let flap.

• Point boat at MOB.

• Ensure main can flap, if not dip downwind.

• Spill and fill main on close reach aiming slightly upwind.

• Retrieve MOB on leeward side.

Retrieval of MOB

With larger keelboats you need to have a method of retrieving people from the water. If they are conscious and not hypothermic use a ladder or foothold, e.g. bowline. Otherwise consider:

- Boarding ladder.
- Detached mainsheet.
- Handy Billy from boom or halyard.
- Parbuckling with small sail.
- Dinghy.
- Helicopter harness or equivalent.

Handling under Power

- At Level 2 keep the power manoeuvres to simple coming alongside and picking up moorings.
- Demonstrate prop wash effect by engaging astern while secured alongside.
- Practise turning boat under power.
- Prepare for coming alongside – observe wind and tide, secure fenders and warps, position crew, communication, boat control, use of springs.

Moorings

- Wind and tide.
- Preparation (boat hook/warp).
- Communication.
- Boat control.

Seamanship Skills

Grounding:

- Lee shore dangers.
- Awareness of state of tide.

If grounding on windward shore:

- Ease or drop main, back jib, heel.

If grounding on lee shore:

- If quick you may be able to sheet in main and tack off. If not, drop main quickly to avoid being blown on further.
- If you have an engine heel boat and motor off.
- With no engine, put out kedge.
- If the tide is falling and no help is available, protect side of boat as it dries.

Emergency steering:

Keelboats can be steered rudderless by lashing the helm exactly amidships and using sail trim and, to some extent, balance as in a dinghy. Emergency steering can involve the use of an oar, a spinnaker pole or boathook, or even a bucket attached to each quarter.

Day Sailing in Keelboats

One day of a Day Sailing Course should be spent undertaking a day passage. Your planning must be first class. The Senior Instructor or Keelboat Instructor is responsible for the safety of the whole group and should not hesitate to change or abandon the plan if weather or other circumstances dictate.

When planning a trip consider the following:

- Weather • Distance • Student preparation – laminated chartlets, notebook
- Tides, streams, tidal gates, heights for entering and leaving harbours or anchorages
- Extra clothing, drink, food • Extra equipment, tow lines, flares • Radio contact, shore contact
- Emergency plan, refuge port • Danger on route, shipping etc. • Landmarks on route, buoys etc.
- Moorings, pontoon, anchorage at destination.

The problem is to give everyone an experience of pilotage rather than following the boat in front. Try to encourage everyone to become involved in the pilotage but avoid splitting the fleet unless there is an instructor in each boat.

Rigging/Launching

- Show students where to sit.
- Demonstrate which items may be used as handholds, and which must not be used.
- Hoist mainsail first.
- Boat must be head to wind to hook on halyard lock (if fitted).
- Tack down haul must not be tensioned yet, nor mainsheet attached.
- Hoist jib and reeve jib sheets if not fitted with a fully furling system.
- Attach rudders and lock up.
- Lift bow and slide trolley under.
- Show students how to hold onto the boat, with one hand on the forestay bridle, the other holding the bow.
- Trolley boat into water and float off.
- Stow trolley ashore.
- Warn students of danger of placing feet under hulls in shallow water.
- Crew holds boat head to wind.
- Helmsman attaches mainsheet.
- Leave windward shore by sailing backwards with the jib furled and rudders up: crew on each hull between bridle and main beam to lift sterns clear.
- Control rate of sternway by backing jib.
- The boat can be steered by lowering the appropriate crew's legs into the water.
- Leave other shores by sailing off gently, lowering windward rudder first.
- When in clear water, stop to lower leeward rudder and tension tack down haul.

Familiarisation

- As for monohulls.
- Give a greater feeling of security.

Orientation/Basic Boat Controls

Orientation is as for monohulls, but there are important differences in the basic boat controls session:

- Point out that multihulls do have brakes – the rudders.
- The mainsail/jib controls used for monohull teaching are very different for multihulls.
- Introduce two traveller positions: upwind/reaching (central) and downwind (out).

Tacking

1. Helm sails close-hauled and looks for a flat patch on the water. Sitting position is back leg bent, front leg straight, tiller over rear shoulder, mainsheet in front hand.

   The helm calls "Ready about". Crew responds "Ready" and uncleats the jib. Helm calls "Lee oh" and eases tiller away so that the rudders are no more than 45 degrees. In strong winds, sheet in hard as the bows approach head-to-wind.

2. Helm moves quickly to the centre of the boat and onto both knees, facing aft. The tiller is swung behind the mainsheet falls.

3. Still facing aft, the helm places the tiller into the new back hand and prepares to face forward. Crew keeps boat flat and moves accordingly. They may back the jib to assist the tack.

4. Helm pivots and sits looking forward, tiller over rear shoulder, mainsheet in front hand. Crew will join them on the windward side and sheet jib correctly.

5. When the battens 'pop' on their new side, the helm releases a metre of mainsheet to help the boat to bear away. Once on the new course, the helm can sheet in and power away.

The Five Essentials:

1. Sail setting – the use of telltales nearest the head of each sail is introduced earlier than in monohull teaching, because of the fully battened mainsail. Introduce the use of the streamer on the forestay bridle as an aid downwind (the streamer should be at 90 degrees to the boat for optimum downwind sailing).

2. Balance – stress the different helmsman/crew positions for light and medium winds.

3. Trim – check that the boat is level by comparing waterlines forward and aft.

4. Centreboard – inappropriate for Darts. Other multihulls may have centreboards used in the same way as in monohulls. Downwind gybing may require small amounts of centreboard for steerage.

5. Course sailed – as for monohulls but emphasise the amount of time lost through inefficient tacking. Also stress the importance of gybing downwind.

Gybing

1. With the boat sailing efficiently on a downwind course, with the mainsail out almost to the shroud and the traveller out at least halfway, the helm calls "Stand by to gybe". Crew responds "Yes" and the helm begins steering away from the wind.

2. The helm immediately moves into the centre of the boat, facing aft, and continues to steer gently. Crew uncleats jib and prepares to move across the boat.

3. The helm, still facing aft, passes the tiller across behind the falls into the new back hand, but continues to steer. Crew prepares to change the jib over

4. The helm takes hold of the mainsheet falls with the new front hand and with a positive movement guides the mainsail through the gybe as the back of the boat passes through the wind.

5. As the mainsail crosses and the battens 'pop', the tiller should be centralised. The crew, having crossed the boat, sheets in on the new side.

6. The helm pivots and sits, looking forward, and steers onto the new course. Once settled, the boat can be powered up and sailed at maximum speed once more.

Coming Ashore

- Lift the leeward rudder first.
- Ease the mainsail tack downhaul and furl jib.
- Sail in slowly with the traveller eased off.
- With an onshore wind the crew can dangle his legs in the water on the windward side, forward of the shroud to slow the boat down.
- Crew sits by main beam and chooses right moment to slide off into the water on windward side to hold boat.
- An alternative for the lee shore landing is for the helm to go head to wind well off shore, drop the mainsail and remove the halyard. Raise the rudders, then both crew sit on the hulls, forward of the main beam and 'steer' the boat as described on page 81.
- For an offshore wind the helmsman lifts the windward rudder when close to shore.

• Meanwhile, the crew sits by the main beam and chooses the right moment to slide carefully off into the water on the windward side to hold the boat again, by the main beam.

• In strong winds with restricted access, the boat is sailed in under jib alone.

Coming ashore on sandy beaches with an onshore wind and large waves, the technique is different and the multihull is the only boat it applies to:

• De-power the mainsail.

• Pick the right area and both helmsman and crew sit aft to keep the bows up.

• At the right moment the helmsman trips the rudders and keeps going straight for the shore.

• Take care when alighting from the boat and turning it head to wind.

Further Sessions

The ability to sail around a triangular course marks an important stage in basic instruction, as it shows that the student can tackle all points of sailing.

Teaching of man overboard recovery (see page 87) differs fundamentally from monohull teaching. Having regained control, the person left aboard will prefer to gybe rather than tack to get back to the man in the water, as it is quicker and the helmsman is in control throughout the manoeuvre. In addition, the man is recovered from between the hulls and if necessary over the main beam, rather than at the shroud.

Teaching Further Skills

Once the basic techniques have been covered in RYA Level 1, 2 and 3 courses, further multihull training follows the syllabi laid down in the RYA National Sailing Scheme Logbook G4, amended as appropriate with specialist techniques.

Capsize Recovery

1. As the boat capsizes, the helm and crew must quickly decide on their route into the water. They should avoid the sails, shrouds and mainsheet. Falling from the top sponson can also be a painful experience.

   Once in the water, as with all capsizes, both crew should remain in contact with the boat. The stern is a convenient place to meet.

2. The helm and crew then climb out onto the lower hull and begin their tasks. The helm releases the mainsheet and traveller, while the crew releases the jib and finds the righting line, usually at the base of the mast.

3. The righting line is thrown over the top hull.

4. Using the righting line, both of the crew can then lean back, using their body weight to begin the righting process. The hull of the boat will have swung downwind of the rig. Consequently, the wind will now be blowing on the trampoline to assist with the righting. However, if this is the case, the crew must be prepared for the boat coming up very quickly.

As the rig releases from the water, the boat will begin to right itself quickly.

5. To deal with this, the crew get ready to move quickly between the hulls and apply their body weight onto the forward crossbeam...

6. ...preventing the boat going right over and re-capsizing. **This action can be reduced by righting the boat head to wind.**

7. Once the boat is righted, the crew can climb back aboard, preferably over the forward crossbeam. Then all sheets and lines can be tidied before sailing away.

Man Overboard

1. For this exercise a target (fender) is used, and dropped in the water. The boat is sailed away on a beam reach and the jib is released with the helm noting the position of the MOB.

2. Once far enough away (15 boat lengths), the helm gybes the boat.

3. The helm then sails back to the MOB on a close reach, noting any drift.

4. Once close to the target, the helm heads up into the wind to slow the boat, aiming to position the MOB between the hulls.

5. If possible, the boat is sailed head to wind. The boat is stopped this way. The rudders can also be put fully over to help stop the boat. The helm then moves forward ready to bring aboard the MOB. It is preferable that the MOB is brought aboard over the forward crossbeam.

SEAMANSHIP SKILLS

Manoeuvres

Many of these are a revision and refinement of skills learnt on a Level 2 course. Nevertheless, during a 2-day course you may only have time to teach the skills required without a great deal of further coaching. Each technique can be broken down into four stages:

- **Planning**
- **Approach**
- **Manoeuvre**
- **Escape**

A briefing and demonstration or land drill ashore can be used for many techniques.

Practice doesn't necessarily make perfect – it may serve only to repeat poor technique and hence reinforce mistakes. That's where you come in.

Ideally, bring all the manoeuvres together once they have been learnt into the framework of a seamanship exercise or a seamanship game.

The principle is to combine the exercises in a way which will make their practice more enjoyable and their execution more efficient. The golden rule about games is to keep them simple. Don't get bogged down in penalty points and the like, the fun will soon evaporate.

If the game is packaged properly, students won't have time to realise that it is simply structured practice. It could be marketed as an obstacle course or treasure hunt full of local interest. It could also be a short triangular course with a different task each lap.

Instructing from a Teaching Boat (Power or Sail)

With many of the topics outlined above, the instructor may first be in the sailing dinghy, but then is most likely to be out of it, allowing the students to practise under supervision. As soon as the instructor gets out of the dinghy, communication problems increase.

Reefing Afloat

Briefing ashore:
- When to reef – purpose.
- Where to reef – away from hazards, starboard tack if possible.
- How – order of events, co-ordination between helm and crew.
- How much – appearance of reefed sail, i.e. efficient shape, boom not drooping, no wrinkles, kicking strap still effective.
- Genoa changed to jib and centreboard raised slightly if necessary.

Progression:
- Sail around a course once reefed.
- 'Timed' reefing/shaking out.
- Reef on the whistle.

Anchoring

Briefing ashore:
- Type of anchor and selection of suitable anchorage.
- Nature of bottom.
- Shelter.
- Depth (changes with tide).
- Length of warp.
- Swinging area.

Practise afloat:

- Approach on close reach or against tidal stream.
- Consider dropping jib if possible to provide a clear foredeck.
- Drop main if wind against tide.
- Ensure the warp passes through fairlead or bow strop.
- Lower anchor when boat stops.
- Payout warp.
- Check holding with transits.
- Stow sails when holding.

Being Towed By a Powerboat

This can be covered best in an informal discussion using the following key points:

- Good communication.
- Approach.
- Pass tow line.
- Drop mainsail.
- Secure tow line.
- Bridle/strong points.
- Quick release system.
- Being towed alongside.
- Springs.
- Being towed stern first.
- Centreboard up.
- Crew weight aft.
- Steer if possible.

Lee Shore Landing

- Approach from well upwind, throw the main halyard overboard and ensure that it streams freely.
- Turn head to wind, ease the kicker, take off the Cunningham, release the main halyard and drop the mainsail fully into the boat, removing the halyard from the headboard of the sail.
- Bear away and head for the beach using the jib for power.
- Prior to arrival, raise the centreboard and release the rudder downhaul.
- In the shallows, release the jib, round up into wind and the crew step out and secure the boat head to wind.

Sailing Without a Rudder (or with an elastic loop over the tiller)

- Raise centreboard to three quarters down.
- Rudder can be raised rather than removed. Alternatively, a thick loose elastic loop allows some tiller movement.
- Consider reefing the mainsail so as not to overpower the jib.
- Jib in, main out to bear away.
- Main in to luff up.
- To sail on a reach in a straight line, sheet the jib correctly then gently sheet in the main to balance its power.
- Boats usually have slight weather helm when both sails are filled.
- If rudder raised keep weight forward.
- Heel to windward to bear away.
- Heel to leeward to luff up.

- Slow movements across the boat, but 'anticipate' the boat's movements.
- Can be easier if jib sheets tied together and mainsheet reeved as a simple purchase.
- Following a gybe keep jib to windward until settled on new course to prevent spinning.

Progression:
- Sail around a windward/leeward course.
- Sail the boat more 'freely' when going upwind.
- Gybe the main deliberately by passing it over.

Sailing Without a Centreboard

- Explain the underwater shape of the boat.
- Heeling to leeward helps upwind progress.
- Lateral resistance can be increased by moving the crew weight forward.

Progression:
- Sail around a windward/leeward course.

Sailing Backwards

- Explain why, which can be escaping from a crowded mooring or leaving a weather shore/jetty.
- Centreboard at least half down.
- Bring the boat head to wind and ensure it is stopped.
- Push the boom swiftly to the shroud so that the mainsail backs.
- As soon as the boat starts to gather leeway, point the tiller away from the boom.
- Steer by looking backwards and keep the rudder movements small (the boat follows the direction that the rudder is pointing).

DAY SAILING

Navigation

- Small boat navigation is really pilotage.
- You cannot do detailed chart work in an open boat.
- Pre-planning is essential.

Charts

- Chart datum.
- Measuring distances from latitude scale.
- Soundings.
- Drying heights.
- Heights above mean high water springs.
- Conspicuous features, lighthouses, headlands etc.
- Common hazards, rocks, wrecks, overfalls etc.

Compass

- Compass rose.
- Variation – corrections.

Tide and Tide Tables

- High and low water.
- Correction for BST.
- Springs and neaps.
- Rule of twelfths/percentage rule.
- Tidal streams and tidal diamonds.

Food, Drink and 'Comfort'

- Suitable clothing. • Harbour regulations. • Avoiding shipping. • Where to moor or beach at destination.
- Shoreside facilities.

Planning and Pilotage

- Sailing a passage, which has first been planned.
- The time available, ETD, ETA, length of any breaks.
- Consideration of tide and weather conditions, traffic etc.
- Use laminated charts and chinagraph pencil.
- Create a 'passage plan' on a separate sheet (easier to look at than a chart).
- Create an expedition sheet including number of participants and other relevant info.
- Establish a shore contact and give them the details.
- Consider informing the Coastguard and/or Harbour master,

Pilotage is usually a visual exercise rather than sailing for long distances on a compass bearing. If you know where you are, with a chart and compass you should be able to identify where to go next.

- Courses, distances and time on chart.
- Sail on transits to avoid being set sideways by tide.
- At known positions e.g. buoys, confirm position or alter course.

Emergencies

- Carry appropriate flares.
- Carry a Marine VHF and mobile phone in a waterproof bag.
- Create a 'Plan B' including alternative safe havens and a plan for darkness.

Meteorology

Sources of weather information:

- Television/Radio – Inshore forecast, local forecast (details in nautical almanac).
- Weather fax/text forecasts by mobile phone/telephone.
- Internet and email forecasts.

Terms used in shipping forecasts:

- Beaufort scale and direction.
- Link that with tidal information to determine likely sea state.
- Backing and veering.
- Good, moderate and poor visibility.

Weather Patterns

- Rapid barometric change usually indicates strong winds.
- Anticlockwise wind circulation around lows.
- Clockwise wind circulation around highs.
- Warm front – lowering cloud, decreasing visibility, drizzle, veering winds.
- Cold front – veer, cooler, more northerly wind, clear, showery, possible sudden squalls.
- Sea breeze – air over warm land rises, cool sea, air drawn ashore.
- Fog – advection: warm air over cool sea, or radiation: land cools.

Observation afloat:

- Squalls • Gusts • Approach of low pressure – cirrus clouds, hazy sun.

Decision Making

- Planning for difficult conditions • Alternative destinations • The effect of wind and tide on sea conditions.

SAILING WITH SPINNAKERS

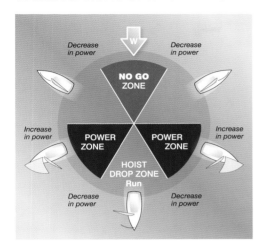

Spinnaker Hoists

There are a number of ways to hoist the spinnaker, depending on the situation.

Symmetric Spinnaker – Leeward Hoist (or Spinnaker Chute Hoist)

Once helm has sailed boat onto training run (hoist drop zone):

1. Crew puts pole on.

Helm hoists spinnaker and balances boat, while steering with tiller between the legs if necessary.

2. Crew takes the guy and cleats, crew then moves to windward side deck.

3. Helm sits in appropriate place to balance boat. Crew takes sheet and adjusts as necessary. Adjust pole height to keep both clews level.

Symmetric Spinnaker – Windward Hoist

1. Crew gathers spinnaker up into a ball and checks that the spinnaker guy is free.

2. Crew throws the spinnaker forward as the helm hoists quickly. In most boats this would require the helm to steer with the tiller between the legs. Communication/co-ordination is very important, otherwise the spinnaker will end up under the bow of the boat.

3. Crew puts pole on whilst helm keeps the spinnaker flying by playing the guy and the sheet.

4. Crew takes the guy and cleats, sitting to windward.

5. Helm sits in appropriate place to balance boat. Crew takes the sheet and adjusts as necessary. Adjust pole to keep both clews level.

Asymmetric Spinnaker – Hoist

1. Helm bears away until the boat is in the hoist/drop zone. (If appropriate, crew passes helm the spinnaker sheet.)

2. Crew launches pole and spinnaker with launch line (some boats use separate lines for each in which case the pole is launched first).

3. Crew hoists spinnaker (if separate).

4. Helm 'powers up' by luffing slightly as crew sheets in.

5. As the boat accelerates the helm bears away and the crew eases the sheet. Communication is paramount to keep the boat achieving maximum VMG (velocity made good) i.e. the crew needs to tell the helm whether the sheet load from the power in the sail is increasing or decreasing. The helm can then steer accordingly. Keep the boat flat by steering towards the mast tip.

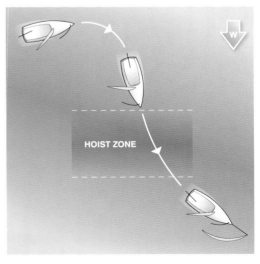

HOIST ZONE

Spinnaker Gybing: Symmetric

Again, there are a number of ways to share jobs during the gybe.

1. As the helm bears away into the hoist/drop zone, the crew brings the pole back with the guy to set the spinnaker for that point of sailing.

2. Helm calls 'Stand by to gybe'. If crew responds 'Yes' then he gybes the mainsail.

3. Crew releases guy from the cleat, stands up and hands sheet and guy to the helm. Crew swaps the pole to the new side whilst the helm balances the boat and plays both the guy and sheet to keep the spinnaker flying.

4. Crew adjusts the new guy and cleats it.

5. Crew then sits on new windward side taking the new sheet. Helm sits to balance the boat. As a development, the crew may gybe the main with the kicker.

Spinnaker Gybing: Asymmetric

1. Choose a good place to gybe when the boat is travelling fast and in clear water. Crew prepares by gathering slack in new sheet.

2. Whilst the helm is bearing away the crew gradually eases the sheet to assist the spinnaker to slide through the slot in front of the jib, then releases the old sheet and begins pulling on the new sheet.

3. Helm bears away into the hoist/drop zone and gybes the main with the mainsheet falls.

4. Helm steers carefully throughout the manoeuvre and into the new hoist/drop zone.

5. Helm will probably have to luff slightly to fill the spinnaker.

6. If necessary, bear away as the boat speed increases, crew trims as required.

Spinnaker Drop (Windward): Symmetric Spinnaker Drop (Bag)

1. Crew hands sheet to helm to keep the spinnaker flying whilst pole is being removed. Helm steers with tiller between legs if necessary.

2. Crew takes the pole off the mast and then off the spinnaker clew and stows it.

3. On the crew's command, the helm releases the spinnaker halyard and the crew pulls the spinnaker down on the windward side, working up the leech first and then along the foot (this reduces the chance of the spinnaker twisting on the next hoist).

4. Crew then stows it in the bag and tidies up the sheets. Meanwhile the helm is looking ahead.

Spinnaker Drop (Windward): Asymmetric Spinnaker Drop

1. Helm bears away into hoist drop zone.

2. Crew hands sheet to helm to keep the spinnaker flying until the drop. (This keeps the boat moving faster and keeps the spinnaker out of the water during the drop).

3. Crew pulls in excess retrieval line (to stop spinnaker going under the bow and to speed up the drop).

4. Crew uncleats halyard and pulls down the spinnaker by its retrieval line. If there are separate launch lines, then the pole must be uncleated first.

5. As this is happening, the helm balances the boat and looks ahead.

START RACING

The course should include the following characteristics:

- An emphasis on racing as fun.
- Ensuring that starts and rules are not intimidating.
- The provision of enough information for Level 2 standard sailors to get round a club racing course safely, without presenting a hazard to other sailors.
- Encouragement to sailors to start racing, join a club and progress within the sport.

The Course and Starting Sequence

Club Course

Most clubs will have fixed buoys with a system to identify them. The course used will depend upon the wind direction on the day. It will normally be posted as a list of buoys in the order they are to be rounded and which side to leave them on (port or starboard) e.g. SL (Start Line), Ep (Leave buoy E to port), Bs (Leave buoy B to starboard). Also outline the number of laps required.

Trapezoid with Outer Loop

Popular open meeting course, especially with youth classes. These types of course are also extremely good when sailing multiple classes on the same course – different loops can be specified for different classes. This keeps the classes apart on the water.

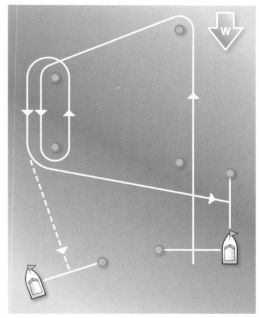

Trapezoid with Inner Loop

Popular open meeting course, as above.

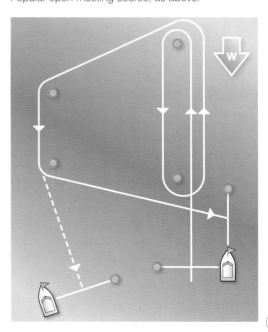

Triangle Sausage Course

Originally called an Olympic triangle, useful with established classes at open meetings and national events.

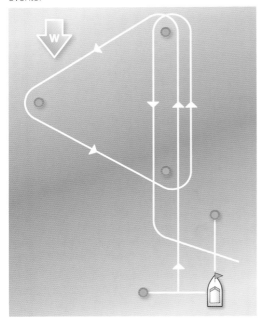

Sausage or Windward/Leeward Course

Very popular with modern asymmetric boats, as they have to go downwind in a series of broad reaches for maximum speed.

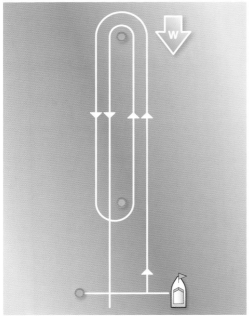

Starting Sequence

The starting system used by the majority of sailing clubs consists of a warning signal, a preparatory signal and a start signal. The flags and sound signals used to draw attention to the starting sequence are shown in G12, the RYA Advanced Sailing Handbook. The most common system is five minute – four minute – one minute – go.

Other signals relating to starting:

Individual Recall

If one or more competitors are over the line at the start then flag X (blue cross against white background) will be displayed immediately after the start with a sound signal. This will be displayed until all competitors have started properly, or up to four minutes after the start, or up to one minute before a following start.

General Recall

If several unidentified boats are over the line at the start then the race will be restarted to ensure fairness. Under these circumstances the First Substitute flag (yellow triangle on a blue triangular background) will be flown with two sound signals. The preparatory signal for the next start will normally be one minute after the First Substitute is lowered.

Starting Penalty Flags

The starting penalty flags are displayed with the preparatory flags and dropped one minute before the start. If any one of these flags is flown then a boat that enters the triangle formed by the two ends of the start line and the first buoy will be penalised as follows:

Flag I – the competitor must sail to the pre-start side of the line by going around either end of the line.

Flag Z – the competitor shall receive a 20% scoring penalty.

Black Flag – the competitor shall be disqualified and shall not be allowed to restart the race if a general recall is necessary.

Boat Tuning

Tuning a boat can vary between knowing when to ease the kicking strap or pull on the Cunningham in a Laser, to adjusting mast rake and altering the spreaders in a Fireball. The best place to start tuning is to find out what other people who race successfully in the class are doing. Most class associations and sail makers publish tuning guides. Class websites are a good place to start.

Before experimenting with any rig settings on a boat it is a good idea to set it up to the class average given in the tuning guides.

Tactics and Strategy

This covers everything from finding the fastest way up the beat using the changes in direction of the wind to manoeuvring at close quarters to gain an advantage on other boats.

Race strategy

This determines the fastest route around the course dependant on the weather, tidal currents, sea state and surrounding land masses.

Tactics

The course you actually take around the race course must take into consideration other boats and the rules that govern fair sailing. These include sailing your boat clear of dirty wind, approaching marks using the rules, overtaking slower boats, etc.

Dirty Wind

The wind to leeward of a dinghy is affected in both strength and direction. To continue on the same tack, to leeward and behind another boat, will result in the boat sailing both lower and slower until it has dropped far enough behind to not be affected.

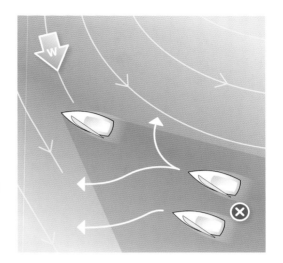

Course Down the Reach

A tactical advantage can be gained by sailing very low at the start of a reach as long as there is a gap behind you to prevent your wind being blanketed by other boats. This technique allows for a fast approach to the next buoy on the inside of boats which have gone high.

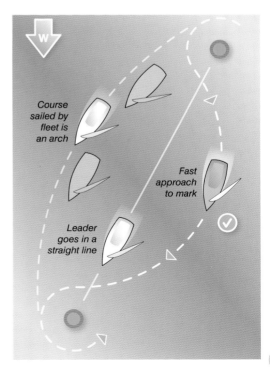

Course sailed by fleet is an arch

Fast approach to mark

Leader goes in a straight line

Using Lifts and Avoiding Headers

By studying the water upwind whilst beating, gusts can be seen as dark areas on the water. Advantages can be gained by preparing the boat for the gusts and altering course to make the best use of them. The wind is constantly changing in direction so one tack will always point a dinghy slightly closer to the next mark than the other – this is the lifted tack.

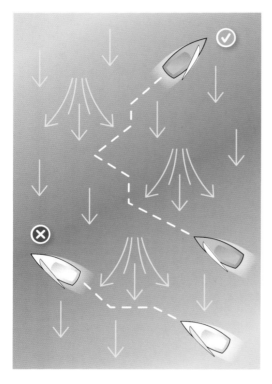

Wind Bends

Where the wind bends there can be a significant advantage in sailing towards the inside of the bend. This should result in the boat sailing a shorter distance, as it will spend more time on a lifted tack.

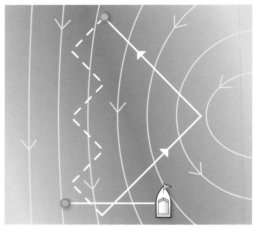

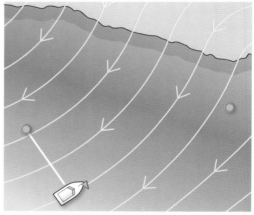

Boat Handling

To be able to apply tactics around the race course good boat handling skills are essential. There are many exercises which concentrate specifically on boat handling, including tacking/gybing on the whistle, follow my leader, start line exercises and racing around a short course.

Videoing sailors can be a useful way to provide feedback, which should focus on the key points of the exercise rather than recording everything.

It is generally accepted that to develop boat handling skills it is important to break down a particular manoeuvre into smaller segments. This enables the sailor to focus on particular areas of improvement.

Simple Rules

Refer to the RYA Handy Guide to the Racing Rules.

Penalties
A boat infringing a rule in part 2 may exonerate itself by taking a penalty. The penalty is to complete a two turns penalty in the same direction at the earliest opportunity. The boat shall have no rights of way during the manoeuvre.

If a boat fouls a mark she may exonerate herself by performing a 1 turn penalty at the earliest opportunity.

It should be noted that both of these penalties are routinely altered by the Sailing Instructions.

Exercises

By far the most important aspect of teaching people to race is actually racing on the water. Many different exercises can be used to develop sailors' understanding and performance around a course. The race can be broken down as follows and specific exercises used to improve performance.

Starting
A good start is measured by: Sailing at maximum speed, in clear air and on or close to the line when the start signal sounds. Starting is a key skill and confidence on the start line is essential if racing is to be enjoyed successfully. Starting exercises should receive major emphasis during a 'Start Racing' Course.

Timing to be near the start line as the gun goes
A simple start line and a short windward leg can be used to practise a number of starts with a short race afterwards. For the purpose of training a shortened two minute – one minute – go is normally used.

Holding position and accelerating
Again, a simple start line and windward leg can be used, but the start sequence should involve the start being sounded 15 seconds or so either side of the normal start signal. This encourages people to practise holding position near the start line and accelerating away at the start signal. One of the problems in training with a small number of boats is that the starts are not very realistic – there is rarely congestion at the start line. Boats can practise these skills by hovering next to a buoy for as long as possible before bearing away with the sails, sheeting, slowing and accelerating to full speed. Sailing backwards can also be a useful skill.

Another useful exercise is 'follow my leader', taking the boats on a close reach and slowing down almost to a standstill before accelerating again.

Line bias
To raise awareness of the line bias the anchor rope on the committee boat can be periodically lengthened and shortened between starts to alter the bias. This will encourage sailors to regularly check the bias of the start line.

Windward leg
Speed upwind
Start the sailors lying-to in a line across the wind, level and in clear air. This compares speed and pointing. Once they have spread out, regroup and start again.

Tactics and lay lines
After a briefing on tactics a number of short races can be run with a finish between the safety boat and the windward mark. Boats should be encouraged to practise tacking on the lay line and covering other boats up the beat whilst protecting their clear air. They should vary their approach to the mark but always on starboard tack and in clear air.

Mark rounding

Practise bearing away

A small triangular or sausage course should be laid with all the boats sailing around it. The safety boat can then be held near the windward mark to offer coaching advice to the boats bearing away. The emphasis should be on heeling the boat slightly to windward and easing the main, to minimise use of the rudder. You should ask them to consider easing the kicker, Cunningham, adjusting the centreboard and, when windy, getting the crew weight back to assist the turn.

Practise gybing

A slalom course can be used to practise reach-to-reach gybing or a whistle to initiate run-to-run gybing.

Tactics

Start the boats at the windward mark of a triangular course, enabling the boats to arrive at the gybe mark close together. This should allow sailors a chance to think ahead and practise good mark rounding. The safety boat should ideally be positioned inside the course near the gybe mark.

Off wind legs

Speed including spinnakers if applicable

Start the boats from 'follow-my-leader' on a beam reach, a good distance upwind of a mark. This will allow the boats an equal start with other boats in close proximity. Focus should be on boat speed alone with the boats not attempting to block the wind of others.

Tactics

A similar exercise can be run but this time with the emphasis on gaining position by covering other boats whilst keeping their own air clear. This can be done on a reach or a run.

More information on the Portsmouth Yardstick is available on the RYA website.

Performance Sailing

Boat Setup

This will include general principles and use of rig controls.

Boat Handling

Including use of symmetric and asymmetric spinnakers, trapezing and safety.

Coaching

Candidates will be encouraged to develop a positive but relaxed style, which brings about improvement in those being coached.

Use of the Powerboat

Safe and effective driving and positioning for coaching and safety.

Advanced Instructor candidates should be familiar with the relevant chapters of G12 Advanced Handbook.

Briefing

The briefing is vitally important because high performance boats could be spread out over a far larger area than a fleet of beginner boats. Make certain of your briefing:

• Clear and concise (use pictures and diagrams).

• Safety and recall signals understood by everyone.

• The session aims are clear.

• The learning objectives are clear and understood by all students. This is especially important in a group of mixed ability.

• The sailing area is suitable for the purpose of the session. Downwind sailing in a breeze will require much more space than roll tacking practice in light winds.

• Use bullet points and don't waffle.

• Use effective questioning to make sure everyone understands what is going to happen on the water.

• Don't try and cover too much in each session – concentrate on 'bite size chunks'.

Land Drills

Due to the nature of the boats and the subject matter involved, the use of land drills is highly recommended. Exercises which can benefit from land drills include:

• Spinnaker hoists, gybes and drops.

• Trapeze work (ensure that they are safe).

• Sail setting and sail controls. This is also an excellent way to make sure that all boats are set up correctly for the conditions.

• Tacking and gybing practice.

Demonstrate and then give the students time to practise, using positive coaching all the time. Take care that no one will get hurt falling off a trapeze onto hard ground or falling out of a dinghy whilst dropping a spinnaker.

Demonstrations

Demonstrations are vital to teach the more complicated advanced skills. This is why it is of paramount importance that you as the Instructor can competently sail performance boats. Areas of coaching that benefit from demonstrations include:

• Tacking and gybing (including rolling).

• Mark rounding.

• Spinnaker hoist, gybe and drop.

Coaching

Effective coaching whilst on the water is one of the most important aspects of becoming an Advanced Instructor. The ability to assess the performance of a dinghy or student and make a valid contribution to their improvement is fundamental to your role.

• Be effective. If you don't have anything useful to say, don't say anything!

• Be positive. Sailing is fun.

• Keep it short and simple. Don't overload your students.

• Try and reduce stress levels, people perform much better if they are relaxed.

• Be precise and don't waffle. Tell them exactly how to improve. For clarity use the same words as you used when briefing where possible.

• Don't try and shout across an expanse of water, get them to stop and come alongside – it saves time in the long run.

• Make notes whilst on the water to assist your debrief.

Top Tip

Consider using a video camera. Students can see exactly the point being made.

Debrief

The debrief is very important as it will probably contain most of the coaching points for improvement. You must give positive feedback from the session on the water. Very often your debrief will be analytical and will deal with a number of small but specific points. It may involve going back to a land drill to demonstrate a point or specific manoeuvre. Always try and involve all of the students and find a positive point for them all.

Debrief points to remember:

• Use the 'Traffic Light' for feedback.

- Be specific.
- Analyse each boat's performance individually and involve all students.
- Relate performance to session aims as well as what happened on the water.
- Be positive. A lot of students will be ecstatic at just having sailed an RS200 with a kite up, so don't pull their performance to pieces!.
- Don't be afraid to go back to a land drill – it will reinforce their learning.
- Remember it's fun. They should want to go back on the water to improve their sailing after the debrief.

Top Tip

When gybing, ensure your students look where they are going and make small adjustments to the helm all the way through – 'Steer through the gybe'.

Safety

Sailing high performance boats always involves capsizing at some point. The ability to capsize, right the dinghy and sail on is an essential skill when racing high performance boats. It is important that you make your students aware of the particular risks which can be involved. Useful issues can include:

- Clothing. Make sure all students have the correct personal equipment required for sailing a performance dinghy: wetsuits or dry suits, good quality gloves, trapeze harness that fits correctly and has a quick release hook if possible, dinghy or wetsuit boots, buoyancy aid that is suitable (i.e. high fit that gives plenty of room for movement).
- Knife. Advise that they should all carry a knife that can be used to cut themselves clear of the boat or equipment. Ensure that the one in the safety boat is easily accessible.
- Run a positive safety briefing before your students go afloat. Don't put your students off, but make them aware of relevant issues on the day:
  1. The lack of an air pocket under many high performance dinghies when inverted
  2. The risk of being caught on rigging with a trapeze harness
  3. The risk of injury during a high-speed wipe-out
  4. Avoiding inversions
- Make sure that all boats being used are safe. Tape up any sharp areas or fittings, make sure that any wire is not fraying, check all fittings and control lines on a regular basis.
- Ascertain the ability of all students before going afloat. You can always increase the challenge, but lost confidence is difficult to replace.

Use mast head flotation. It's not 'cool', but it eliminates inversions which are energy sapping to recover.

TECHNIQUE AND SKILL

One way of looking at how the theory becomes practice is to consider that the RYA Method discussed later in this book is the component part of the RYA Skills Model shown below, and that practice by the student using training exercises shapes those components and develops the techniques to become more skilful.

Technique – The physical movements that make up a manoeuvre.
Skill – The ability to perform a technique appropriate to the conditions at will and consistently while under pressure. Right skill, right time, right place.

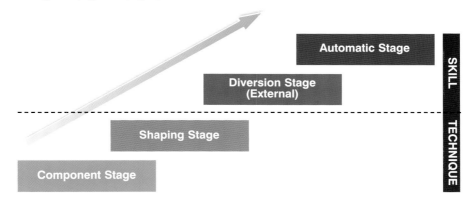

RYA SKILLS MODEL

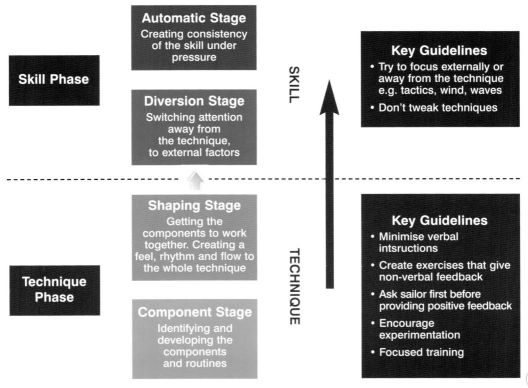

13 | Teaching Disabled Sailors

Teaching a disabled person to sail is exactly like teaching a non-disabled person. You mix common sense with experience and apply safe practice.

The overall objective is to learn how to sail effectively, develop confidence, enjoyment, a sense of achievement and to have fun. It is important to encourage maximum participation and activity by people. Do not prejudge a person's competence by their disability, but rather by their experience, knowledge and ability. The first thing you should do is ask!

We are all individuals each with different interests. Someone with a disability has ideas, makes plans, gets excited, even bloody minded. There is no need to adopt a different manner and vocabulary or to feel sympathy or embarrassment. The important thing is to treat a disabled person as you would anyone else.

A disability is not a barrier to the successful completion of courses. All participants must be able to demonstrate their ability to complete the whole syllabus, but this can be achieved by proxy. A candidate who cannot perform a task directly must be able to satisfactorily direct a third party to achieve that task on their behalf. It is worth bearing in mind that the candidate has to possess good communication and teaching skills as well as knowing how to undertake the manoeuvre.

The 'special endorsements' line of the course completion certificate should be treated with care. Do not list any disability unless it directly affects the holder's ability to handle a boat, so the prosthesis that gives a user complete function is of no consequence. However, a visually impaired person may have the endorsement 'Requires visual assistance on the water'.

How RYA Sailability can Support your Training Needs

Attitudes to the inclusion of disabled people in sport are forever changing, but we know that the biggest barriers of all are the concerns of non-disabled people. The barriers that these concerns create are often born of ignorance and apprehension, but most significantly from a lack of awareness.

Without the numerous club members and RYA Sailability volunteers there would be no support to organise so many sailing opportunities throughout the country. As groups expand and new ones start up the demand for volunteers grows.

Disabled people want to go sailing and often need a variety of support to enable them to do so. Some are totally independent: others may need help with transport, launching boats etc. Volunteers do not have to be a sailor or paramedic to help someone get afloat, every job is important, but it is essential to identify what job is best for them.

RYA Sailability offers training packages that can support your groups/clubs in both awareness and volunteer organisation.

RYA Sailability Awareness Training

RYA Sailability Awareness is a comprehensive training course that will allow and encourage helpers to become involved by alleviating their fear of disability and give them the knowledge needed to enjoy their involvement to the full. The course covers the following:

- The needs of sailors with disabilities, both ashore and afloat.
- Improved communication skills.
- The use of current terminology to explain disability.
- The use of specialist equipment and adaptations.
- Moving, handling and transfer techniques.
- Courses are held throughout the UK.
  To find out about your nearest course please contact RYA Sailability www.rya.org.uk/sailability 0844 5569550.

Communication is the key to success

It is essential that communication is a two way process. Key points to remember are:

- Never assume.
- Ask.
- Listen.
- Establish individual communication.
- Emphasise the ability not disability.
- Make the terminology/jargon clear.
- Build trust.
- Check understanding.
- Offer empathy not sympathy.
- Learn very basic sign language.

Part of the skill of an instructor or coach is to be able to teach from a powerboat, which is why Powerboat Level 2 and Safety Boat awards are necessary for Instructors, Senior Instructors and racing coaches.

Always wear the kill cord, attached securely to your leg. If you then fall overboard, the boat will stop and not endanger others.

Instead of shouting from a moving powerboat to a moving sailing boat, tell the students to stop and lie-to before approaching the boat slowly from the windward side. Alternatively, overtake the boat to windward but on a parallel course. Stop the boat and offer advice as they sail past. Keep the propeller away from people and ropes at all times.

A capsized boat should always be approached bow-to (techniques are given in G16 Safety Boat Handbook).

Take care when approaching the shore to keep clear of people in the water and avoid damage to the propeller.

Always be prepared to take boats in tow and have a routine worked out in advance for leaving shore (windward or leeward) and returning to shore (windward or leeward). The use of anchors and holding moorings are particularly useful.

ADVANCED TRAINING

The best strategy when teaching more advanced skills is usually to float free or anchor, calling boats over for input when required. However, you may wish to observe and coach boats sailing at high speeds. Constant vigilance is essential. The ability to drive a powerboat well and control its position in relation to a fast moving dinghy is a skill that only comes with a lot of practice. Whilst on the water, even though you may have half a dozen boats in your group, you will often be working in a one to one scenario and then moving on to the next boat whilst the others practise.

Specific points regarding coaching from a moving powerboat:

- ALWAYS have the kill cord attached. A RIB travelling at speed with no driver is extremely dangerous.
- Tracking near a fast moving dinghy on a parallel course is sometimes required in a coaching context to observe and provide feedback. The priority is that the powerboat should be positioned in such a way that if a mishap occurs with the dinghy or its crew, the helm of the powerboat can take the appropriate avoiding action.
- Communicating on the move is difficult, so stop the powerboat with the engine off and have the dinghy come alongside.
- Once alongside, a dinghy with racks or wings can 'rest' them on the side of the powerboat. This is sometimes called the 'secure lie-to'.
- Types of powerboat – most performance boats are fairly fragile so RIBs with console steering are the best choice. Beware if it has a lighting frame.
- Depending on the session, position the coach boat in the correct place to enable effective coaching. These are:

  1. Tacking exercise: coach boat to leeward of the fleet.
  2. Gybing exercise: coach boat to windward of the fleet.
  3. Windward mark rounding: coach boat to windward of the mark.
  4. Leeward mark rounding: coach boat to windward of the mark or use coach boat as the leeward mark.
  5. Trapezing, spinnaker work or boat speed exercise: following individual boats at a safe distance (see above).
  6. Starting practice: coach boat at windward end of the line and on the line.

- If using a camera, it is highly recommended that someone else drives the boat if it is going to be under way with the engine running.

> **Top Tip**
>
> Always wear the kill cord.
>
> Keep the propeller away from people in the water.
>
> During an incident, count heads first.
>
> Stop the engine on arrival if there is someone in the water.

MARK LAYING FOR TRAINING COURSES

When running single handed, improvers or racing sessions, you will need to lay a succession of short, easily moved courses. To avoid problems, remember the following points:

- Keep marks as simple as possible.
- Avoid complicated systems with blocks and weights: sinkers are cheaper and less trouble than anchors.
- Always lay marks over the windward side of your teaching boat.
- Have the warp flaked, with the sinker on top ready to go. Retrieve marks in the same way.
- Re-flake neatly as you haul in.
- Don't use warps which float (polypropylene).
- A short length of chain 1m below the mark will help prevent it being 'picked up' by a rudder/daggerboard if a student rounds too closely.
- A range of marks of different colours makes identification easier.
- It is sometimes easier to lay a mark in approximately the right place, and then tow it into its exact position. Sinkers make this easier than anchors.
- Have a simple communication system if working with a mother ship or committee boat.
- Move a course after large wind shifts.

RYA CODE OF CONDUCT FOR INSTRUCTORS, TRAINERS AND COACHES

Sports training and coaching helps the development of individuals through improving their performance.

This is achieved by:

- Identifying and meeting the needs of individuals.
- Improving performance through a progressing programme of safe, guided practice, measured performance and/or competition.
- Creating an environment in which individuals are motivated to maintain participation and improve performance.

Instructors, Trainers and Coaches should comply with the principles of good practice listed below. They must:

- If working with young people under the age of 18, have read and understood the Child Protection Policy as detailed on the RYA website at www.rya.org.uk under Information and Advice.
- Respect the rights, dignity and worth of every person and treat everyone equally within the context of their sport.
- Place the well-being and safety of the student above the development of performance. They should follow all guidelines laid down by the RYA and hold appropriate insurance cover.
- Develop an appropriate working relationship with students (especially children), based on mutual trust and respect and not exert undue influence to obtain personal benefit or reward. In particular, they must not abuse their position of trust to establish or pursue a sexual relationship with a student aged under 18, or an inappropriate relationship with any student.
- Encourage and guide students to accept responsibility for their own behaviour and performance.
- Hold relevant up to date and nationally recognised governing body qualifications.
- Ensure that the activities they direct or advocate are appropriate for the age, maturity, experience and ability of the individual.
- At the outset, clarify with students (and where appropriate their parents) exactly what is expected of them and what they are entitled to expect.
- Always promote the positive aspects of their sport (e.g. courtesy to other water users).
- Consistently display high standards of behaviour and appearance.

SAFEGUARDING AND CHILD PROTECTION

Introduction

RYA Recognised Training Centres are required to have a formal child protection policy which is checked as part of their annual inspection. Your organisation is therefore strongly advised to take the following steps.

Adopt a policy statement that defines the organisation's commitment to providing a safe environment for children.

Produce a simple code of practice and procedures governing how the organisation runs.

The RYA publishes guidelines to help clubs, training centres and instructors to enable children and vulnerable adults to enjoy the sports of sailing, windsurfing and power boating in all their forms, in a safe environment. They can be copied or adapted to meet the requirements of the organisation. The document and other best practice guidance can be downloaded from the RYA's website www.rya.org.uk/go/childprotection.

The RYA Policy Statement on Child Protection is as follows:

As defined in the Children Act 1989, for the purposes of this policy anyone under the age of 18 should be considered as a child. The policy also applies to vulnerable adults.

It is the policy of the RYA to safeguard children and young people taking part in boating from physical, sexual or emotional harm. The RYA will take all reasonable steps to ensure that, through appropriate procedures and training, children participating in RYA activities do so in a safe environment. We recognise that the safety and welfare of the child is paramount and that all children, whatever their age, gender, disability, culture, ethnic origin, colour, religion or belief, social status or sexual identity, have a right to protection from abuse.

The RYA actively seeks to:

- Create a safe and welcoming environment, both on and off the water, where children can have fun and develop their skills and confidence.
- Support and encourage recognised training centres, affiliated clubs and class associations to implement similar policies.
- Recognise that safeguarding children is the responsibility of everyone, not just those who work with children.
- Ensure that RYA-organised training and events are run to the highest possible safety standards.
- Be prepared to review its ways of working to incorporate best practice.

We will:

- Treat all children with respect and celebrate their achievements.
- Carefully recruit and select all employees, contractors and volunteers.
- Respond swiftly and appropriately to all complaints and concerns about poor practice or suspected or actual child abuse.

This policy relates to all employees, contractors and volunteers who work with children or vulnerable adults in the course of their RYA duties. It will be kept under periodic review. All relevant concerns, allegations, complaints and their outcome should be notified to the RYA Child Protection Co-ordinator.

NOTE FOR PRINCIPALS – Good Recruitment Practice

If a good recruitment policy is adopted, and the issue of child protection covered in the organisation's risk assessment and operating procedures, both children and adults should be adequately protected. Potential abusers have difficulty operating in a well-run organisation. All applications, whether for paid or voluntary work, should be subject to an appropriate level of scrutiny. The level of checking you carry out should be proportionate to the role and the level of risk involved. The risk may be higher if the person will be in regular contact with the same child or children, in sole charge of children with no parents or other adults present, and/or in a role involving authority and trust, such as an instructor or coach.

The organisation should agree a clear policy and apply it fairly and consistently.
Consider:

- Who to check
- The level of check to be conducted for each category
    - References.
    - Self-disclosure.
    - Enhanced Criminal Records Disclosure (and Barred List Check, if appropriate), or PVG Scheme Membership (Scotland).

Criminal Records Disclosures

Organisations affiliated to or recognised by the RYA can access the Disclosure process through the RYA. The procedure varies according to the home country and legal jurisdiction in which your organisation is located. Full up to date information is available from the RYA website, or contact the RYA's Safeguarding Co-ordinator.

GOOD PRACTICE GUIDELINES

Culture

It is important to develop a culture within your organisation where both children and adults feel able to raise concerns, knowing that they will be taken seriously, treated confidentially and will not make the situation worse for themselves or others. Some children may be more vulnerable to abuse or find it more difficult to express their concerns. For example, a disabled child who relies on a carer to help them get changed may worry that they won't be able to sail any more if they report the carer. A child who has experienced racism may find it difficult to trust an adult from a different ethnic background.

Minimising risk

Plan the work of the organisation and promote good practice to minimise situations where adults are working unobserved or could take advantage of their position of trust. Good practice protects everyone – children, volunteers and staff. These common sense guidelines should be available to everyone within your organisation.

- Avoid spending any significant time working with children in isolation.
- Do not take children alone in a car, however short the journey.
- Do not take children to your home as part of your organisation's activity.
- Where any of these are unavoidable, ensure that they only occur with the full knowledge and consent of someone in charge of the organisation or the child's parents.
- Design training programmes that are within the ability of the individual child.
- If a child is having difficulty with a wetsuit or buoyancy aid, ask them to ask a friend to help if at all possible.
- If you do have to help a child, make sure you are in full view of others, preferably another adult.

You should never:

- Engage in rough, physical or sexually provocative games.
- Allow or engage in inappropriate touching of any form.
- Allow children to use inappropriate language unchallenged, or use such language yourself when with children.
- Make sexually suggestive comments to a child, even in fun.
- Fail to respond to an allegation made by a child – always act.
- Do things of a personal nature that children can do for themselves.

It may sometimes be necessary to do things of a personal nature for children, particularly if they are very young or disabled. These tasks should only be carried out with the full understanding and consent of both the child (where possible) and their parents/carers. In an emergency situation which requires this type of help, parents should be fully informed. In such situations it is important to ensure that any adult present is sensitive to the child and undertakes personal care tasks with the utmost discretion.

Responsibilities of Staff and Volunteers

Staff or volunteers should be given clear roles and responsibilities. They should be aware of your organisation's child protection policy and procedures and be given guidelines on:

- Following good practice.
- Recognising signs of abuse (see RYA Guidelines).

Identifying Child Abuse

The following brief notes provide a guide to help you identify signs of possible abuse and know what action to take in such cases. The RYA Safeguarding and Child Protection Guidelines on the RYA website cover the subject more fully.

Forms of Abuse

Abuse and neglect are forms of maltreatment of a child. Somebody may abuse or neglect a child by inflicting harm, or by failing to act to prevent harm. Children may be abused in a family or in an institutional or community setting, by those known to them or, more rarely, by a stranger. They may be abused by an adult or adults, or another child or children.

Physical abuse may involve adults or other children causing physical harm:

- by hitting, shaking, squeezing, biting or burning, giving children alcohol, inappropriate drugs or poison, attempting to suffocate or drown children
- in sport situations, physical abuse might also occur when the nature and intensity of training exceeds the capacity of the child's immature and growing body.

Neglect is the persistent failure to meet a child's basic physical and/or psychological needs, likely to result in the serious impairment of the child's health or development.

- neglect in a sailing situation might occur if an instructor or coach fails to ensure that children are safe, or exposes them to undue cold or risk of injury.

Sexual abuse involves an individual forcing or enticing a child or young person to take part in sexual activities, whether or not the child is aware of what is happening, to meet their own sexual needs. The activities may involve:

- actual physical contact or encouraging children to behave in sexually inappropriate ways
- showing children pornographic books, photographs, videos or online images or taking pictures of children for pornographic purposes
- sport situations which involve physical contact (eg. supporting or guiding children) could potentially create situations where sexual abuse may go unnoticed. Abusive situations may also occur if adults misuse their power over young people.

Emotional abuse is the persistent emotional maltreatment of a child such as to cause severe and persistent adverse effects on the child's emotional development.

- emotional abuse in sport might include situations where parents or coaches subject children to constant criticism, bullying or pressure to perform at a level that the child cannot realistically be expected to achieve.

Some level of emotional abuse is involved in all types of maltreatment of a child.

Bullying (including cyberbullying) may be seen as deliberately hurtful behaviour, usually repeated or sustained over a period of time, where it is difficult for those being bullied to defend themselves. The bully may often be another young person. Although anyone can be the target of bullying, victims are typically shy, sensitive and perhaps anxious or insecure. Sometimes they are singled out for physical reasons – being overweight, physically small, having a disability or belonging to a different race, faith or culture.

Recognising Signs of Possible Abuse

It is not always easy, even for the most experienced carers, to spot when a child has been abused. However, some of the more typical symptoms which should trigger your suspicions would include:

- Unexplained or suspicious injuries such as bruising, cuts or burns, particularly if situated on a part of the body not normally prone to such injuries.
- Sexually explicit language or actions.
- A sudden change in behaviour (e.g. becoming very quiet, withdrawn or displaying sudden outbursts of temper).
- The child describes what appears to be an abusive act involving him/her.
- A change observed over a long period of time (e.g. the child losing weight or becoming increasingly dirty or unkempt).
- A general distrust and avoidance of adults, especially those with whom a close relationship would be expected.
- An unexpected reaction to normal physical contact.
- Difficulty in making friends or abnormal restrictions on socialising with others.

It is important to note that a child could be displaying some or all of these signs, or behaving in a way which is worrying, without this necessarily meaning that the child is being abused. Similarly, there may not be any signs, but you may just feel that something is wrong.

Listening to the Child

Children may confide in adults they trust, in a place where they feel at ease.

Always:

- Stay calm – ensure that the child is safe and feels safe.
- Show and tell the child that you are taking what he/she says seriously.
- Reassure that child and stress that he/she is not to blame.
- Be careful about physical contact, it may not be what the child wants.
- Be honest, explain that you will have to tell someone else to help stop the alleged abuse.
- Make a record of what the child has said as soon as possible after the event.
- Follow your organisation's child protection procedures.

Never:

- Rush into actions that may be inappropriate.
- Make promises you cannot keep (e.g. you won't tell anyone).
- Ask more questions than are necessary for you to be sure that you need to act.
- Take sole responsibility – consult someone else (ideally the designated Child Protection/Welfare Officer or the person in charge or someone you can trust) so that you can begin to protect the child and gain support for yourself.

What to do if you are concerned about a child or about the behaviour of a member of staff:

A complaint, concern or allegation may come from a number of sources: a child, their parents or someone within your organisation. It may involve the behaviour of one of your volunteers, employees, or an incident relating to the child at home or at school. Allegations can range from mild verbal bullying to physical or sexual abuse.

If you have noticed a change in the child's behaviour, first talk to the parents or carers. It may be that something has occurred, such as a bereavement, which has caused the child to be unhappy. However if there are concerns about sexual abuse or violence in the home, talking to the parents or carers might put the child at greater risk.

It is NOT your responsibility to investigate further; however, it is your responsibility to act on your concerns and report them to the organisation's Child Protection/Welfare Officer or person in charge, who will make the decision to contact Children's Services or the Police and report to the RYA Safeguarding Co-ordinator. There are simple flow diagrams in the RYA Guidelines that take you through the actions to be taken.

If you have concerns regarding the behaviour of a member of staff or volunteer, inform the organisation's designated Child Protection/Welfare Officer or the person in charge, who should follow the RYA's procedures. It may become necessary for the member of staff to be temporarily suspended while an investigation takes place.

It is important to understand that a member of staff reporting suspicions of child abuse, particularly by a colleague, may undergo a very high degree of stress, including feelings of guilt for having reported the matter. It is therefore very important to ensure that appropriate counselling and support is available for staff.

INSTRUCTOR COURSE AND ENDORSEMENT LOG

Assessment Standards

All RYA-qualified Instructors and Assessors are required to treat students and candidates with respect and fairness. They also have a duty of care.

All instructor assessments in the use of boats and their equipment have implications for the safety of future sailing scheme participants. It is therefore essential that instructor candidates be given a thorough and searching assessment. It would be dangerous to the instructor candidate and anyone whom they subsequently teach if a Coach/Assessor erred on the side of leniency in awarding an instructor certificate. There must never be any question of relaxing the standards required for an instructor award.

Realistic Aims

In some cases, it becomes clear to the Coach/Assessor at an early stage in the assessment process that the candidate has been over-ambitious in their choice of award. In such instances the Coach/Assessor should discuss the situation with the candidate and agree revised achievable aims.

Grounds for Appeal

A candidate has grounds for appeal if he or she believes:

That they have not been given a reasonable opportunity to demonstrate their competence.

Or

That the person carrying out the assessment has placed them under undue or unfair pressure.

Or

That the Coach/Assessor has reached the wrong conclusion on the basis of the outcome of the candidate's performance in the assessment.

The Procedure

The candidate should first raise the concern with the Coach/Assessor to see if the matter can be amicably resolved. If it is inappropriate to consult the Coach/Assessor, or if there is no amicable solution, the candidate should appeal in writing to the RYA National Sailing Coach within 20 working days of the assessment. The letter of appeal should contain the following:

- Full details of the assessment – when, where, involving whom etc.
- The nature of the appeal.
- Any supporting documentation relating to the assessment – outcome, action plans, reports etc.

On receipt of an appeal, an investigative process will commence. Following investigation, the candidate will be informed of the outcome, which will be one of the following:

- The original decision confirmed.
- The assessment carried out again by the same or a different Coach/Assessor.
- The original decision overturned and the assessment judged to be adequate.

If the candidate is still unhappy about the decision, they may appeal against the outcome to the RYA Training Committee.

AVOIDING COMPLAINTS

Most complaints arise from a lack of communication.

- After passing a course, students often wish to attend further modules.
- They usually haven't done any practice in between, so won't have the skill to pass.
- This should be recognised at the point of booking and appropriate alternatives offered. If not, the instructor will need to do the adjusting and guiding.
- Fortunately, due to the scheme being modular, different skills, experience and abilities can be catered for.

The purpose of the scheme remains to teach sailing and improve people's skills and techniques.

- If the module is inappropriate the instructor should discuss realistic aims and gain agreement using tact and diplomacy.
- Struggling students are often relieved by this process.
- Performance often improves once the stress has been removed.
- Ensure students are kept informed with regular debriefs.
- Try to spot 'serial' complainers early.
- Counter them by running the course 'by the book'.
- Regularly ask them if they are satisfied, would like any further input and seek agreement. The Principal or Chief Instructor should also give opportunities for feedback as the course progresses.
- Any complaints received should be referred to the SI, Chief Instructor/Principal (in that order).
- Begin with 'Thank you for bringing this to our attention, how can we resolve it?'
- Often, more tuition is all that's required. It can save a lot of correspondence afterwards.

If you do not inform people of their progress you are more likely to receive a complaint along the lines of "I didn't achieve the certificate because I wasn't taught well."

The instructors who receive the fewest complaints are those who are competent, take an interest in their students, and ensure that even the difficult or weak students feel they are an important part of the group. The instructional skills required are well beyond those of just sailing or even just teaching.

MANUAL HANDLING

Manual handling is any transporting or supporting of a load (including the lifting, putting down, pushing, pulling, carrying or moving thereof) by hand or bodily force.

As an Instructor it is worth being aware that workplace injuries can affect your life and recreation as well as your work, particularly in later years. Injuries sustained while sailing can also affect your students.

This includes sudden injuries in the workplace as well as cumulative wear and tear, commonly caused by poor positioning over a period of time.

Common risks arise from:

- Excessive or awkward loads for one person.
- Slippery or uneven surfaces.
- Repetition or excessive duration of tasks.

Slipways, jetties and dragging boats can all give rise to these circumstances. Studies show that the overwhelming proportion of accidents in the workplace are sprains or strains due to manual handling. Of these, back injuries are three times more common than any other injury.

The Manual Handling Operations Regulations 1992 contain guidance suggesting that manual handling should be included in risk assessments and that employers, employees and volunteers should take sensible steps to minimise the risks.

Top Tip

Handling tips for instructors:

1. Widen the base of support whilst lifting/carrying.
2. Keep the load inside the base of support whenever possible.
3. Avoid asymmetry, e.g. carrying a heavy fuel can.
4. In general before lifting:

ASSESS: task, load, environment, individual(s).

PLAN: task, route.

PREPARE: load, self, area.

Finally, when it comes to moving boats, ensure you have sufficient people to carry out the task safely e.g. pulling a heavy dinghy up a steep slipway.

16 | Logbook

| DATE | LOCATION | HOURS' EXPERIENCE | | ACTIVITY AND WEATHER CONDITIONS | | AUTHORISATION |
		ROLE	HOURS	TYPE OF COURSE OR ACTIVITY	MAX WIND SPEED	SIGNATURE/ NAME

DATE	LOCATION	HOURS' EXPERIENCE		ACTIVITY AND WEATHER CONDITIONS		AUTHORISATION
		ROLE	HOURS	TYPE OF COURSE OR ACTIVITY	MAX WIND SPEED	SIGNATURE/ NAME

17 | Recommendations for Coaching Awards

ASSISTANT INSTRUCTOR

Training and assessment record
The candidate:

Principal's initials

Is aware of safety requirements

Is aware of teaching sequence used when teaching beginners

Is aware of the teaching points for each part of the sequence

Is proficient in teaching shore drills

Is proficient in teaching capsize recovery

The candidate has demonstrated competence as an Assistant Instructor to the standards laid down by the RYA,

Signed (RYA Principal)

Name in capitals

Recognised Training Centre

Date

INSTRUCTOR COURSE AND ENDORSEMENT LOG

The following Instructor Course and Endorsement Log is a record of course completion and NOT a qualification. This book should always be supported by an Instructor Certificate which will be issued on receipt of notification from the RYA Course Coach/Assessor. Please note it is also a requirement for instructors to hold a valid first aid certificate of a type approved by the RYA, and a Powerboat Level 2 certificate before progressing to the instructor training course.

RYA DINGHY/KEELBOAT/MULTIHULL/INSTRUCTOR

Pre-entry Assessment Completed

Venue	COASTAL/INLAND
Date	
Type of boat	DINGHY/KEELBOAT/MULTIHULL
Approved by (RYA Coach/Assessor)	*Signature*
Name in capitals	

Training Course Completed

Venue	COASTAL/INLAND
Date	
RYA Coach/Assessor	*Signature*
Name in capitals	
Moderator	*Signature*
Name in capitals	

Assessment/Moderation Completed

I confirm that the candidate has demonstrated competence as an Instructor in a DINGHY/KEELBOAT/MULTIHULL (delete as appropriate) to the standards laid down by the RYA.

Venue	
Date	
Approved by (RYA Coach/Assessor)	*Signature*
Name in captals	

ADVANCED INSTRUCTOR ENDORSEMENT

Endorsement Completed

I confirm that the candidate has demonstrated competence as an Advanced Instructor to the standards laid down by the RYA.

Venue

COASTAL/INLAND

Date

Approved by (RYA Coach/Assessor)

Signature

Name in capitals

KEELBOAT INSTRUCTOR ENDORSEMENT

Endorsement Completed

I confirm that the candidate has demonstrated competence as a Keelboat Instructor to the standards laid down by the RYA.

Venue

COASTAL/INLAND

Date

Approved by (RYA Coach/Assessor)

Signature

Name in capitals

MULTIHULL INSTRUCTOR ENDORSEMENT

Endorsement Completed

I confirm that the candidate has demonstrated competence as a Multihull Instructor to the standards laid down by the RYA.

Venue

COASTAL/INLAND

Date

Approved by (RYA Coach/Assessor)

Signature

Name in capitals

DINGHY INSTRUCTOR ENDORSEMENT

(For those whose initial instructor award is in keelboats or multihulls)

Endorsement Completed

I confirm that the candidate has demonstrated competence as a Dinghy Instructor to the standards laid down by the RYA.

Venue   COASTAL/INLAND

Date

Approved by (RYA Coach/Assessor)
                                                         Signature

Name in capitals

RACING INSTRUCTOR ENDORSEMENT

Endorsement Completed

I confirm that the candidate has demonstrated competence as a Racing Instructor to the standards laid down by the RYA.

Venue   COASTAL/INLAND

Date

Approved by (RYA Coach/Assessor)
                                                         Signature

Name in capitals

SENIOR INSTRUCTOR

Recommendation

I confirm that the candidate is competent to plan, organise and run a course within the RYA National Sailing Scheme.

Signature (Principal) — *Signature*

Name in capitals

Recognised Training Centre

Date

Training Course

I confirm that the candidate has successfully completed the course and has demonstrated competence in all the areas required.

Venue — COASTAL/INLAND

Date

RYA Coach/Assessor 1 — *Signature*

Name in capitals

RYA Coach/Assessor 2 — *Signature*

Name in capitals

COACH/ASSESSOR

Recommendation

I confirm that the candidate has the experience and technical competence to be trained as a Coach/Assessor with the RYA National Sailing Scheme.

Regional Development Officer/Coach

Signature

Name in capitals

Training Course

I confirm that the candidate has successfully completed the course and has demonstrated competence in all the areas required.

RYA HQ Training Chief Instructor

Signature

Name in capitals

Details of dates, venue and conditions must be entered in the Personal Log on page 115.

Task Experience

I confirm that the candidate has assisted with an RYA Instructor Course and Assessment.

RYA Coach/Assessor

Signature

Name in capitals

The candidate has completed all the requirements and is hereby appointed as an RYA Coach/Assessor.

RYA HQ Training Chief Instructor

Signature

Date

ABACK	The sail pressed backwards by the wind.
ABAFT	Behind the boat.
ABEAM	At right angles to the line of the boat.
ADRIFT	Afloat, but without a propulsive force.
AFT	Towards back of the boat.
AGROUND	On the ground and not afloat.
AHEAD	The area in front of the boat.
AMIDSHIPS	In the middle of the boat.
AWASH	The boat being full of water.
BACKING	The wind changing direction in an anti-clockwise direction (against the sun).
BALANCE	How level the boat is.
BEAM	The side of a boat.
BEARING AWAY	Changing direction away from the wind.
BELAY	Twist a rope around something to make fast.
BELLY OF THE SAIL	The fullness of the sail.
BIGHT	A loop.
BLANKETING	To take the wind from another craft which is to leeward.
BOTTLE SCREW	A means of attaching and adjusting shrouds.
BROACHING	To turn sideways onto the wind and heel over.
BURGEE	A flag.
BY THE LEE	Sailing with the wind on the same side of the boat as the mainsail.
CABLE	A nautical measurement being 200 yards or 100 fathoms.
CARS	Adjustable fairleads on tracks, to adjust sheet angle.
CASTING OFF	Leaving the moorings.
CATSPAWS	Ripples on the surface of the water showing a gust of wind.
CHAIN PLATE	Metal plate to which the shrouds are attached at their base.
CLAWING OFF	Sailing off a lee shore.
COAMING	The built up woodwork around hatches etc to exclude water.
CRINGLE	The metal ring used to reinforce any holes in the sail.
CROSS TREES	Horizontal spreaders which hold the shrouds away from the mast.
CUNNINGHAM	System for tensioning luff of sail.
DISPLACEMENT	The amount of water that a boat displaces (Archimedes' Principle).
DOWNHAUL	See Cunningham.
EASE, TO	To slacken.

EBB	A tide is on the ebb when it is falling.
EDDY	A current flowing in a different direction to the main stream.
FAIRLEADS	Permanent fixtures on a boat which are designed to guide a rope.
FAIRWAY	A clear passage for navigation.
FALL	The loose end of a rope.
FATHOM	A measurement of depth (1 fathom = 6 feet).
FLOOD	A flooding tide is a rising one.
FREEBOARD	The amount of boat above the water line.
GHOSTING	To move when there is no recognisable wind.
GNAV	Lever above boom, function same as kicker.
HEADWAY	Forward momentum.
HEAT SEALING	Tidy end of rope by melting together.
HOUNDS	The fixture of the mast to which the shrouds are attached.
IN IRONS, STAYS	The boat lies head to wind, sails flapping.
JURY RIG	This is an emergency rig, having undergone temporary repair.
KICKER	(Kicking strap) pulley system between boom and mast designed to tension leech of sail.
LUFF	To change the boat's direction towards the wind.
MAKE FAST	To secure.
MAST STEP	The slot into which the mast heel fits.
OUTHAUL	System for tensioning foot of sail.
RACKS	Metal or carbon extensions to side of boat.
RAKE	Angle of mast to vertical.
ROCKER	Amount of curve on the longitudinal axis at bottom of boat.
SPLICE	To tidy end of rope by weaving through itself.
TELL TALE	Wool or lightweight tape used to detect airflow.
TRIM	Fore and aft adjustment of weight in boat.
VANG	See KICKER.
VEERING	The wind changing direction in a clockwise direction (with the sun).
WARP	Rope used for anchoring or mooring.
WEIGHING	Raising the anchor.
WHIPPING	End of rope tidied by winding twine around it.